THE
BIRTH OF TRAGEDY

OR

HELLENISM AND PESSIMISM

THE BIRTH OF TRAGEDY

OR

HELLENISM AND PESSIMISM

BY

FRIEDRICH NIETZSCHE

TRANSLATED BY

WM. A. HAUSSMANN, PH.D.

KALPAZ

ISBN: 978-93-5128-375-1 (HB)

First Published in 1909
Indian Reprint in 2017

Published by

Kalpaz Publications
C-30, Satyawati Nagar,
Delhi – 110052
E-mail: kalpaz@hotmail.com
Website: kalpazpublications.com
Ph.: +91-9212142040

Cataloging in Publication Data—DK
Courtesy: D.K. Agencies (P) Ltd. <docinfo@dkagencies.com>

Nietzsche, Friedrich Wilhelm, 1844-1900, **author.**
[Geburt der Trago˜die. English]
The birth of tragedy, or, Hellenism and pessimism / by Friedrich Nietzsche ; translated by Wm. A. Haussmann (Ph.D.).
pages cm
Translated from German.
Translation of: Die Geburt der Trago˜die, oder, Griechentum und Pessimismus.
"First published in 1909"
ISBN 9789351283751 (HB)

1. Aesthetics. 2. Music—Philosophy and aesthetics. 3. Tragedy. 4. Greek drama (Tragedy)—History and criticism—Theory, etc. 5. Mythology, Greek, in literature. 6. Tragic, The. I. Haussmann, William A., translator. II. Title. III. Title: Hellenism and pessimism.

B3313.G42E54 2017 DDC 193 23

Contents

INTRODUCTION*

Frederick Nietzsche was born at Röcken near Lützen, in the Prussian province of Saxony, on the 15th of October 1844, at 10 a.m. The day happened to be the anniversary of the birth of Frederick-William IV., then King of Prussia, and the peal of the local church-bells which was intended to celebrate this event, was, by a happy coincidence, just timed to greet my brother on his entrance into the world. In 1841, at the time when our father was tutor to the Altenburg Princesses, Theresa of Saxe-Altenburg, Elizabeth, Grand Duchess of Olden-burg, and Alexandra, Grand Duchess Constantine of Russia, he had had the honour of being presented to his witty and pious sovereign. The meeting seems to have impressed both parties very favourably; for, very shortly after it had taken place, our father received his living at Röcken "by supreme command." His joy may well be imagined, therefore, when a first son was born to him on his beloved and august patron's birthday, and at the christening ceremony he spoke as follows:—"Thou blessed month of October!—for many years the most decisive events in my life have occurred within thy thirty-one days, and now I celebrate the greatest and most glorious of them all by baptising my little boy! O blissful moment! O exquisite festival! O unspeakably holy duty! In the Lord's name I bless thee!—With all my heart I utter these words: Bring me this, my beloved child, that I may consecrate it unto the Lord. My son, Frederick William, thus shalt thou be named on earth, as a memento of my royal benefactor on whose birthday thou wast born!"

Our father was thirty-one years of age, and our mother not quite nineteen, when my brother was born. Our mother, who was the daughter of a clergyman, was good-looking and healthy, and was one of a very large family of sons and daughters. Our paternal grandparents, the Rev. Oehler and his wife, in Pobles, were typically healthy people. Strength, robustness, lively dispositions, and a cheerful outlook on life, were among the qualities which every one was pleased to observe in them. Our grandfather Oehler was a bright, clever man, and quite the old style of comfortable country parson, who thought it no sin to go hunting. He scarcely had a day's illness in his life, and would certainly not

---

* This Introduction by E. Förster-Nietzsche, which appears in the front of the first volume of Naumann's Pocket Edition of Nietzsche, has been translated and arranged by Mr A. M. Ludovici.

have met with his end as early as he did—that is to say, before his seventieth year—if his careless disregard of all caution, where his health was concerned, had not led to his catching a severe and fatal cold. In regard to our grandmother Oehler, who died in her eighty-second year, all that can be said is, that if all German women were possessed of the health she enjoyed, the German nation would excel all others from the standpoint of vitality. She bore our grandfather eleven children; gave each of them the breast for nearly the whole of its first year, and reared them all It is said that the sight of these eleven children, at ages varying from nineteen years to one month, with their powerful build, rosy cheeks, beaming eyes, and wealth of curly locks, provoked the admiration of all visitors. Of course, despite their extraordinarily good health, the life of this family was not by any means all sunshine. Each of the children was very spirited, wilful, and obstinate, and it was therefore no simple matter to keep them in order. Moreover, though they always showed the utmost respect and most implicit obedience to their parents—even as middle-aged men and women—misunderstandings between themselves were of constant occurrence. Our Oehler grandparents were fairly well-to-do; for our grandmother hailed from a very old family, who had been extensive land-owners in the neighbourhood of Zeitz for centuries, and her father owned the baronial estate of Wehlitz and a magnificent seat near Zeitz in Pacht. When she married, her father gave her carriages and horses, a coachman, a cook, and a kitchenmaid, which for the wife of a German minister was then, and is still, something quite exceptional. As a result of the wars in the beginning of the nineteenth century, however, our great-grandfather lost the greater part of his property.

Our father's family was also in fairly comfortable circumstances, and likewise very large. Our grandfather Dr. Nietzsche (D.D. and Superintendent) married twice, and had in all twelve children, of whom three died young. Our grandfather on this side, whom I never knew, must certainly have been a distinguished, dignified, very learned and reserved man; his second wife—our beloved grandmother—was an active-minded, intelligent, and exceptionally good-natured woman. The whole of our father's family, which I only got to know when they were very advanced in years, were remarkable for their great power of self-control, their lively interest in intellectual matters, and a strong sense of family unity, which manifested itself both in their splendid readiness to help one another and in their very excellent relations with each other. Our father was the youngest son, and, thanks to his uncommonly lovable disposition, together with other gifts, which only tended to become more marked as he grew older, he was quite the favourite of the family. Blessed with a thoroughly sound constitution, as all averred who knew him at the convent-school in Rossleben, at the University, or later at the ducal court of Altenburg, he was tall and slender, possessed an undoubted gift for poetry and real musical talent, and was moreover a man of delicate sensibilities, full of consideration for his whole family, and distinguished in his manners.

My brother often refers to his Polish descent, and in later years he even instituted research-work with the view of establishing it, which met with partial success. I know nothing definite concerning these investigations, because a large number of valuable documents were unfortunately destroyed after his breakdown in Turin. The family tradition was that a certain Polish nobleman Nicki (pronounced Nietzky) had obtained the special favour of Augustus the Strong, King of Poland, and had received the rank of Earl from him. When, however, Stanislas Leszcysski the Pole became king, our supposed ancestor became involved in a conspiracy in favour of the Saxons and Protestants. He was sentenced to death; but, taking flight, according to the evidence of the documents, he was ultimately befriended by a certain Earl of Brühl, who gave him a small post in an obscure little provincial town. Occasionally our aged aunts would speak of our great-grandfather Nietzsche, who was said to have died in his ninety-first year, and words always seemed to fail them when they attempted to describe his handsome appearance, good breeding, and vigour. Our ancestors, both on the Nietzsche and the Oehler side, were very long-lived. Of the four pairs of great-grandparents, one great-grandfather reached the age of ninety, five great-grandmothers and-fathers died between eighty two and eighty-six years of age, and two only failed to reach their seventieth year.

The sorrow which hung as a cloud over our branch of the family was our father's death, as the result of a heavy fall, at the age of thirty-eight. One night, upon leaving some friends whom he had accompanied home, he was met at the door of the vicarage by our little dog. The little animal must have got between his feet, for he stumbled and fell backwards down seven stone steps on to the paving-stones of the vicarage courtyard. As a result of this fall, he was laid up with concussion of the brain, and, after a lingering illness, which lasted eleven months, he died on the 30th of July 1849. The early death of our beloved and highly-gifted father spread gloom over the whole of our childhood. In 1850 our mother withdrew with us to Naumburg on the Saale, where she took up her abode with our widowed grandmother Nietzsche; and there she brought us up with Spartan severity and simplicity, which, besides being typical of the period, was quite *de rigeur* in her family. Of course, Grand-mamma Nietzsche helped somewhat to temper her daughter-in-law's severity, and in this respect our Oehler grandparents, who were less rigorous with us, their eldest grandchildren, than with their own children, were also very influential. Grandfather Oehler was the first who seems to have recognised the extraordinary talents of his eldest grandchild.

From his earliest childhood upwards, my brother was always strong and healthy; he often declared that he must have been taken for a peasant-boy throughout his childhood and youth, as he was so plump, brown, and rosy. The thick fair hair which fell picturesquely over his shoulders tended somewhat to modify his robust appearance. Had he not possessed those wonderfully beautiful, large, and expressive eyes, however, and had he not been so very ceremonious in his manner, neither his teachers nor his relatives would ever have noticed anything at all remarkable about the boy; for he was both modest and reserved.

He received his early schooling at a preparatory school, and later at a grammar school in Naumburg. In the autumn of 1858, when he was fourteen years of age, he entered the Pforta school, so famous for the scholars it has produced. There, too, very severe discipline prevailed, and much was exacted from the pupils, with the view of inuring them to great mental and physical exertions. Thus, if my brother seems to lay particular stress upon the value of rigorous training, free from all sentimentality, it should be remembered that he speaks from experience in this respect. At Pforta he followed the regular school course, and he did not enter a university until the comparatively late age of twenty. His extraordinary gifts manifested themselves chiefly in his independent and private studies and artistic efforts. As a boy his musical talent had already been so noticeable, that he himself and other competent judges were doubtful as to whether he ought not perhaps to devote himself altogether to music. It is, however, worth noting that everything he did in his later years, whether in Latin, Greek, or German work, bore the stamp of perfection—subject of course to the limitation imposed upon him by his years. His talents came very suddenly to the fore, because he had allowed them to grow for such a long time in concealment. His very first performance in philology, executed while he was a student under Ritschl, the famous philologist, was also typical of him in this respect, seeing that it was ordered to be printed for the *Rheinische Museum.* Of course this was done amid general and grave expressions of doubt; for, as Dr. Ritschl often declared, it was an unheard-of occurrence for a student in his third term to prepare such an excellent treatise.

Being a great lover of out-door exercise, such as swimming, skating, and walking, he developed into a very sturdy lad. Rohde gives the following description of him as a student: with his healthy complexion, his outward and inner cleanliness, his austere chastity and his solemn aspect, he was the image of that delightful youth described by Adalbert Stifter.

Though as a child he was always rather serious, as a lad and a man he was ever inclined to see the humorous side of things, while his whole being, and everything he said or did, was permeated by an extraordinary harmony. He belonged to the very few who could control even a bad mood and conceal it from others. All his friends are unanimous in their praise of his exceptional evenness of temper and behaviour, and his warm, hearty, and pleasant laugh that seemed to come from the very depths of his benevolent and affectionate nature. In him it might therefore be said, nature had produced a being who in body and spirit was a harmonious whole: his unusual intellect was fully in keeping with his uncommon bodily strength.

The only abnormal thing about him, and something which we both inherited from our father, was short-sightedness, and this was very much aggravated in my brother's case, even in his earliest schooldays, owing to that indescribable anxiety to learn which always characterised him. When one listens to accounts given by his friends and schoolfellows, one is startled by the multiplicity of his studies even in his schooldays.

In the autumn of 1864, he began his university life in Bonn, and studied philology and theology; at the end of six months he gave up theology, and in the autumn of 1865 followed his famous teacher Ritschl to the University of Leipzig. There he became an ardent philologist, and diligently sought to acquire a masterly grasp of this branch of knowledge. But in this respect it would be unfair to forget that the school of Pforta, with its staff of excellent teachers—scholars that would have adorned the chairs of any University—had already afforded the best of preparatory trainings to any one intending to take up philology as a study, more particularly as it gave all pupils ample scope to indulge any individual tastes they might have for any particular branch of ancient history. The last important Latin thesis which my brother wrote for the Landes-Schule, Pforta, dealt with the Megarian poet Theognis, and it was in the rôle of a lecturer on this very subject that, on the 18th January 1866, he made his *first appearance in public* before the philological society he had helped to found in Leipzig. The paper he read disclosed his investigations on the subject of Theognis the moralist and aristocrat, who, as is well known, described and dismissed the plebeians of his time in terms of the heartiest contempt The aristocratic ideal, which was always so dear to my brother, thus revealed itself for the first time. Moreover, curiously enough, it was precisely *this* scientific thesis which was the cause of Ritschl's recognition of my brother and fondness for him.

The whole of his Leipzig days proved of the utmost importance to my brother's career. There he was plunged into the very midst of a torrent of intellectual influences which found an impressionable medium in the fiery youth, and to which he eagerly made himself accessible. He did not, however, forget to discriminate among them, but tested and criticised the currents of thought he encountered, and selected accordingly. It is certainly of great importance to ascertain what those influences precisely were to which he yielded, and how long they maintained their sway over him, and it is likewise necessary to discover exactly when the matured mind threw off these fetters in order to work out its own salvation.

The influences that exercised power over him in those days may be described in the three following terms: Hellenism, Schopenhauer, Wagner. His love of Hellenism certainly led him to philology; but, as a matter of fact, what concerned him most was to obtain a wide view of things in general, and this he hoped to derive from that science; philology in itself, with his splendid method and thorough way of going to work, served him only as a means to an end.

If Hellenism was the first strong influence which already in Pforta obtained a sway over my brother, in the winter of 1865-66, a completely new, and therefore somewhat subversive, influence was introduced into his life with Schopenhauer's philosophy. When he reached Leipzig in the autumn of 1865, he was very downcast; for the experiences that had befallen him during his one year of student life in Bonn had deeply depressed him. He had sought at first to adapt himself to his surroundings there, with the hope of ultimately elevating them to his lofty views on things; but both these efforts proved vain, and now he had come to Leipzig with the purpose of framing his own manner of life. It can easily be imagined how the first reading of Schopenhauer's *The World as Will and Idea* worked upon this man, still stinging from the bitterest experiences and disappointments. He writes: "Here I saw a mirror in which I espied the world, life, and my own nature depicted with frightful grandeur." As my brother, from his very earliest childhood, had always missed both the parent and the educator through our father's untimely death, he began to regard Schopenhauer with almost filial love and respect. He did not venerate him quite as other men did; Schopenhauer's *personality* was what attracted and enchanted him. From the first he was never blind to the faults in his master's system, and in proof of this we have only to refer to an essay he wrote in the autumn of 1867, which actually contains a criticism of Schopenhauer's philosophy.

Now, in the autumn of 1865, to these two influences, Hellenism and Schopenhauer, a third influence was added—one which was to prove the strongest ever exercised over my brother—and it began with his personal introduction to Richard Wagner. He was introduced to Wagner by the latter's sister, Frau Professor Brockhaus, and his description of their first meeting, contained in a letter to Erwin Rohde, is really most affecting. For years, that is to say, from the time Billow's arrangement of *Tristan and Isolde* for the pianoforte, had appeared, he had already been a passionate admirer of Wagner's music; but now that the artist himself entered upon the scene of his life, with the whole fascinating strength of his strong will, my brother felt that he was in the presence of a being whom he, of all modern men, resembled most in regard to force of character.

Again, in the case of Richard Wagner, my brother, from the first, laid the utmost stress upon the man's personality, and could only regard his works and views as an expression of the artist's whole being, despite the fact that he by no means understood every one of those works at that time. My brother was the first who ever manifested such enthusiastic affection for Schopenhauer and Wagner, and he was also the first of that numerous band of young followers who ultimately inscribed the two great names upon their banner. Whether

Schopenhauer and Wagner ever really corresponded to the glorified pictures my brother painted of them, both in his letters and other writings, is a question which we can no longer answer in the affirmative. Perhaps what he saw in them was only what he himself wished to be some day.

The amount of work my brother succeeded in accomplishing, during his student days, really seems almost incredible. When we examine his record for the years 1865-67, we can scarcely believe it refers to only two years' industry, for at a guess no one would hesitate to suggest four years at least. But in those days, as he himself declares, he still possessed the constitution of a bear. He knew neither what headaches nor indigestion meant, and, despite his short sight, his eyes were able to endure the greatest strain without giving him the smallest trouble. That is why, regardless of seriously interrupting his studies, he was so glad at the thought of becoming a soldier in the forthcoming autumn of 1867; for he was particularly anxious to discover some means of employing his bodily strength.

He discharged his duties as a soldier with the utmost mental and physical freshness, was the crack rider among the recruits of his year, and was sincerely sorry when, owing to an accident, he was compelled to leave the colours before the completion of his service. As a result of this accident he had his first dangerous illness.

While mounting his horse one day, the beast, which was an uncommonly restive one, suddenly reared, and, causing him to strike his chest sharply against the pommel of the saddle, threw him to the ground. My brother then made a second attempt to mount, and succeeded this time, notwithstanding the fact that he had severely sprained and torn two muscles in his chest, and had seriously bruised the adjacent ribs. For a whole day he did his utmost to pay no heed to the injury, and to overcome the pain it caused him; but in the end he only swooned, and a dangerously acute inflammation of the injured tissues was the result. Ultimately he was obliged to consult the famous specialist, Professor Volkmann, in Halle, who quickly put him right.

In October 1868, my brother returned to his studies in Leipzig with double joy. These were his plans: to get his doctor's degree as soon as possible; to proceed to Paris, Italy, and Greece, make a lengthy stay in each place, and then to return to Leipzig in order to settle there as a privat docent. All these plans were, however, suddenly frustrated owing to his premature call to the University of Bale, where he was invited to assume the duties of professor. Some of the philological essays he had written in his student days, and which were published by the *Rheinische Museum,* had attracted the attention of the Educational Board at Bale. Ratsherr Wilhelm Vischer, as representing this body, appealed to Ritschl for fuller information. Now Ritschl, who had early recognised my brother's extraordinary talents, must have written a letter of such enthusiastic praise ("Nietzsche is a genius: he can do whatever he chooses to put his mind to"), that one of the more cautious members of the council is said to have observed: "If the proposed candidate be really such a genius, then it were better did we not appoint him; for, in any case, he would only stay a short time at the little University of Bale." My brother ultimately accepted the appointment, and, in view of his published philological works, he was immediately granted the doctor's degree by the University of Leipzig. He was twenty-four years and six months old when he took up his position as professor in Bale,—and it was with a heavy heart that he proceeded there, for he knew "the golden period of untrammelled activity" must cease. He was, however, inspired by the deep wish of being able "to transfer to his pupils some of that Schopenhauerian earnestness which is stamped on the brow of the sublime man." "I should like to be something more than a mere trainer of capable philologists: the present generation of teachers, the care of the growing broods,—all this is in my mind. If we must live, let us at least do so in such wise that others may bless our life once we have been peacefully delivered from its toils."

When I look back upon that month of May 1869, and ask both of friends and of myself, what the figure of this youthful University professor of four-and-twenty meant to the world at that time, the reply is naturally, in the first place: that he was one of Ritschl's best pupils; secondly, that he was an exceptionally capable exponent of classical antiquity with a brilliant career before him; and thirdly, that he was a passionate adorer of Wagner and Schopenhauer. But no one has any idea of my brother's independent attitude to the science he had selected, to his teachers and to his ideals, and he deceived both himself and us when he passed as a "disciple" who really shared all the views of his respected master.

On the 28th May 1869, my brother delivered his inaugural address at Bale University, and it is said to have deeply impressed the authorities. The subject of the address was "Homer and Classical Philology."

Musing deeply, the worthy councillors and professors walked homeward. What had they just heard? A young scholar discussing the very justification of his own science in a cool and philosophically critical spirit! A man able to impart so much artistic glamour to his subject, that the once stale and arid study of philology suddenly struck them—and they were certainly not impressionable men—as the messenger of the gods: "and just as the Muses descended upon the dull and tormented Boeotian peasants, so philology comes into a world full of gloomy colours and pictures, full of the deepest, most incurable woes, and speaks to men comfortingly of the beautiful and brilliant godlike figure of a distant, blue, and happy fairyland."

"We have indeed got hold of a rare bird, Herr Ratsherr," said one of these gentlemen to his companion, and the latter heartily agreed, for my brother's appointment had been chiefly his doing.

Even in Leipzig, it was reported that Jacob Burckhardt had said: "Nietzsche is as much an artist as a scholar." Privy-Councillor Ritschl told me of this himself, and then he added, with a smile: "I always said so; he can make his scientific discourses as palpitatingly interesting as a French novelist his novels."

"Homer and Classical Philology"—my brother's inaugural address at the University—was by no means the first literary attempt he had made; for we have already seen that he had had papers published by the *Rheinische Museum*; still, this particular discourse is important, seeing that it practically contains the programme of many other subsequent essays. I must, however, emphasise this fact here, that neither "Homer and Classical Philology," nor *The Birth of Tragedy,* represents a beginning in my brother's career. It is really surprising to see how very soon he actually began grappling with the questions which were to prove the problems of his life. If a beginning to his intellectual development be sought at all, then it must be traced to the years 1865-67 in Leipzig. *The Birth of Tragedy,* his maiden attempt at book-writing, with which he began his twenty-eighth year, is the last link of a long chain of developments, and the first fruit that was a long time coming to maturity. Nietzsche's was a polyphonic nature, in which the most different and apparently most antagonistic talents had come together. Philosophy, art, and science—in the form of philology, then—each certainly possessed a part of him. The most wonderful feature—perhaps it might even be called the real Nietzschean feature—of this versatile creature, was the fact that no eternal strife resulted from the juxtaposition of these inimical traits, that not one of them strove to dislodge, or to get the upper hand of, the others. When Nietzsche renounced the musical career, in order to devote himself to philology, and gave himself up to the most strenuous study, he did not find it essential completely to suppress his other tendencies: as before, he continued both to compose and derive pleasure from music, and even studied counterpoint somewhat seriously. Moreover, during his years at Leipzig, when he consciously gave himself up to philological research, he began to engross himself in Schopenhauer, and was thereby won by philosophy for ever. Everything that could find room took up its abode in him, and these juxtaposed factors, far from interfering with one another's existence, were rather mutually fertilising and stimulating. All those who have read the first volume of the biography with attention must have been struck with the perfect way in which the various impulses in his nature combined in the end to form one general torrent, and how this flowed with ever greater force in the direction of *a single goal.* Thus science, art, and philosophy developed and became ever more closely related in him, until, in *The Birth of Tragedy,* they brought forth a "centaur," that is to say, a work which would have been an impossible achievement to a man with only a single, special talent. This polyphony of different talents, all coming to utterance together and producing the richest and boldest of harmonies, is the fundamental feature not only of Nietzsche's early days, but of his whole development. It is once again the artist, philosopher, and man of science, who as one man in later years, after many wanderings, recantations, and revulsions of feeling, produces that other and rarer Centaur of highest rank—*Zarathustra*.

The Birth of Tragedy requires perhaps a little explaining—more particularly as we have now ceased to use either Schopenhauerian or Wagnerian terms of expression. And it was for this reason that five years after its appearance, my brother wrote an introduction to it, in which he very plainly expresses his doubts concerning the views it contains, and the manner in which they are presented. The kernel of its thought he always recognised as perfectly correct; and all he deplored in later days was that he had spoiled the grand problem of Hellenism, as he understood it, by adulterating it with ingredients taken from the world of most modern ideas. As time went on, he grew ever more and more anxious to define the deep meaning of this book with greater precision and clearness. A very good elucidation of its aims, which unfortunately was never published, appears among his notes of the year 1886, and is as follows:—

"Concerning *The Birth of Tragedy.*—A book consisting of mere experiences relating to pleasurable and unpleasurable æsthetic states, with a metaphysico-artistic background. At the same time the confession of a romanticist *the sufferer feels the deepest longing for beauty—he begets it*; finally, a product of youth, full of youthful courage and melancholy.

"Fundamental psychological experiences: the word 'Apollonian' stands for that state of rapt repose in the presence of a visionary world, in the presence of the world of *beautiful appearance* designed as a deliverance from *becoming*; the word *Dionysos,* on the other hand, stands for strenuous becoming, grown self-conscious, in the form of the rampant voluptuousness of the creator, who is also perfectly conscious of the violent anger of the destroyer.

"The antagonism of these two attitudes and the *desires* that underlie them. The first-named would have the vision it conjures up *eternal*: in its light man must be quiescent, apathetic, peaceful, healed, and on friendly terms with himself and all existence; the second strives after creation, after the voluptuousness of wilful creation, *i.e.* constructing and destroying. Creation felt and explained as an instinct would be merely the unremitting inventive action of a dissatisfied being, overflowing with wealth and living at high tension and high pressure,—of a God who would overcome the sorrows of existence by means only of continual changes and transformations,—appearance as a transient and momentary deliverance; the world as an apparent sequence of godlike visions and deliverances.

"This metaphysico-artistic attitude is opposed to Schopenhauer's one-sided view which values art, not from the artist's standpoint but from the spectator's, because it brings salvation and deliverance by means of the joy produced by unreal as opposed to the existing or the real (the experience only of him who is suffering and is in despair owing to himself and everything existing).—Deliverance in the *form* and its eternity (just as Plato may have pictured it, save that he rejoiced in a complete subordination of all too excitable sensibilities, even in the idea itself). To this is opposed the second point of view—art regarded as a phenomenon of the artist, above all of the musician; the torture of being obliged to create, as a Dionysian instinct.

"Tragic art, rich in both attitudes, represents the reconciliation of Apollo and Dionysos. Appearance is given the greatest importance by Dionysos; and yet it will be denied and cheerfully denied. This is directed against Schopenhauer's teaching of *Resignation* as the tragic attitude towards the world.

"Against Wagner's theory that music is a means and drama an end.

"A desire for tragic myth (for religion and even pessimistic religion) as for a forcing frame in which certain plants flourish.

"Mistrust of science, although its ephemerally soothing optimism be strongly felt; the 'serenity' of the theoretical man.

"Deep antagonism to Christianity. Why? The degeneration of the Germanic spirit is ascribed to its influence.

"Any justification of the world can only be an *æsthetic* one. Profound suspicions about morality (—it is part and parcel of the world of appearance).

"The happiness of existence is only possible as the happiness derived from appearance. (*'Being' is a fiction invented by those who suffer from becoming.*)

"Happiness in becoming is possible only in the *annihilation* of the real, of the 'existing,' of the beautifully visionary,—in the pessimistic dissipation of illusions:—with the annihilation of the most beautiful phenomena in the world of appearance, Dionysian happiness reaches its zenith."

The Birth of Tragedy is really only a portion of a much greater work on Hellenism, which my brother had always had in view from the time of his student days. But even the portion it represents was originally designed upon a much larger scale than the present one; the reason probably being, that Nietzsche desired only to be of service to Wagner. When a certain portion of the projected work on Hellenism was ready and had received the title *Greek Cheerfulness,* my brother happened to call upon Wagner at Tribschen in April 1871, and found him very low-spirited in regard to the mission of his life. My brother was very anxious to take some decisive step to help him, and, laying the plans of his great work on Greece aside, he selected a small portion from the already completed manuscript—a portion dealing with one distinct side of Hellenism,—to wit, its tragic art. He then associated Wagner's music with it and the name Dionysos, and thus took the first step towards that world-historical view through which we have since grown accustomed to regard Wagner.

From the dates of the various notes relating to it, *The Birth of Tragedy* must have been written between the autumn of 1869 and November 1871—a period during which "a mass of æsthetic questions and answers" was fermenting in Nietzsche's mind. It was first published in January 1872 by E. W. Fritsch, in Leipzig, under the title *The Birth of Tragedy out of the Spirit of Music.* Later on the title was changed to *The Birth of Tragedy, or Hellenism and Pessimism.*

ELIZABETH FORSTER-NIETZSCHE.

WEIMAR, September 1905.

AN ATTEMPT AT SELF-CRITICISM

I.

Whatever may lie at the bottom of this doubtful book must be a question of the first rank and attractiveness, moreover a deeply personal question,—in proof thereof observe the time in which it originated, *in spite* of which it originated, the exciting period of the Franco-German war of 1870-71. While the thunder of the battle of Wörth rolled over Europe, the ruminator and riddle-lover, who had to be the parent of this book, sat somewhere in a nook of the Alps, lost in riddles and ruminations, consequently very much concerned and unconcerned at the same time, and wrote down his meditations on the *Greeks,*—the kernel of the curious and almost inaccessible book, to which this belated prologue (or epilogue) is to be devoted. A few weeks later: and he found himself under the walls of Metz, still wrestling with the notes of interrogation he had set down concerning the alleged "cheerfulness" of the Greeks and of Greek art; till at last, in that month of deep suspense, when peace was debated at Versailles, he too attained to peace with himself, and, slowly recovering from a disease brought home from the field, made up his mind definitely regarding the "Birth of Tragedy from the Spirit of *Music."*—From music? Music and Tragedy? Greeks and tragic music? Greeks and the Art-work of pessimism? A race of men, well-fashioned, beautiful, envied, life-inspiring, like no other race hitherto, the Greeks—indeed? The Greeks were *in need* of tragedy? Yea—of art? Wherefore—Greek art?...

We can thus guess where the great note of interrogation concerning the value of existence had been set. Is pessimism *necessarily* the sign of decline, of decay, of failure, of exhausted and weakened instincts?—as was the case with the Indians, as is, to all appearance, the case with us "modern" men and Europeans? Is there a pessimism of *strength*? An intellectual predilection for what is hard, awful, evil, problematical in existence, owing to well-being, to exuberant health, to *fullness* of existence? Is there perhaps suffering in overfullness itself? A seductive fortitude with the keenest of glances, which *yearns* for the terrible, as for the enemy, the worthy enemy, with whom it may try its strength? from whom it is willing to learn what "fear" is? What means *tragic* myth to the Greeks of the best, strongest, bravest era? And the prodigious phenomenon of the Dionysian? And that which was born thereof, tragedy?—And again: that of which tragedy died, the Socratism of morality, the dialectics, contentedness and cheerfulness of the theoretical man—indeed? might not this very Socratism be a sign of decline, of weariness, of disease, of anarchically disintegrating instincts? And the "Hellenic cheerfulness" of the later Hellenism merely a glowing sunset? The Epicurean will *counter* to pessimism merely a precaution of the sufferer? And science itself, our science—ay, viewed as a symptom of life, what really signifies all science? Whither, worse still, *whence*—all science? Well? Is scientism perhaps only fear and evasion of pessimism? A subtle defence against—*truth!* Morally speaking, something like falsehood and cowardice? And, unmorally speaking, an artifice? O Socrates, Socrates, was this perhaps *thy* secret? Oh mysterious ironist, was this perhaps thine—irony?...

2.

What I then laid hands on, something terrible and dangerous, a problem with horns, not necessarily a bull itself, but at all events a *new* problem: I should say to-day it was the *problem of science* itself—science conceived for the first time as problematic, as questionable. But the book, in which my youthful ardour and suspicion then discharged themselves—what an *impossible* book must needs grow out of a task so disagreeable to youth. Constructed of nought but precocious, unripened self-experiences, all of which lay close to the threshold of the communicable, based on the groundwork of *art*—for the problem of science cannot be discerned on the groundwork of science,—a book perhaps for artists, with collateral analytical and retrospective aptitudes (that is, an exceptional kind of artists, for whom one must seek and does not even care to seek ...), full of psychological innovations and artists' secrets, with an artists' metaphysics in the background, a work of youth, full of youth's mettle and youth's melancholy, independent, defiantly self-sufficient even when it seems to bow to some authority and self-veneration; in short, a firstling-work, even in every bad sense of the term; in spite of its senile problem, affected with every fault of youth, above all with youth's prolixity and youth's "storm and stress": on the other hand, in view of the success it had (especially with the great artist to whom it addressed itself, as it were, in a duologue, Richard Wagner) a *demonstrated* book, I mean a book which, at any rate, sufficed "for the best of its time." On this account, if for no other reason, it should be treated with some consideration and reserve; yet I shall not altogether conceal how disagreeable it now appears to me, how after sixteen years it stands a total stranger before me,—before an eye which is more mature, and a hundred times more fastidious, but which has by no means grown colder nor lost any of its interest in that self-same task essayed for the first time by this daring book,—*to view science through the optics of the artist, and art moreover through the optics of life....*

3.

I say again, to-day it is an impossible book to me,—I call it badly written, heavy, painful, image-angling and image-entangling, maudlin, sugared at times even to femininism, uneven in tempo, void of the will to logical cleanliness, very convinced and therefore rising above the necessity of demonstration, distrustful even of the *propriety* of demonstration, as being a book for initiates, as "music" for those who are baptised with the name of Music, who are united from the beginning of things by common ties of rare experiences in art, as a countersign for blood-relations *in artibus.*—a haughty and fantastic book, which from the very first withdraws even more from the *profanum vulgus* of the "cultured" than from the "people," but which also, as its effect has shown and still shows, knows very well how to seek fellow-enthusiasts and lure them to new by-ways and dancing-grounds. Here, at any rate—thus much was acknowledged with curiosity as well as with aversion—a *strange*voice spoke, the disciple of a still "unknown God," who for the time being had hidden himself under the hood of the scholar, under the German's gravity and disinclination for dialectics, even under the bad manners of the Wagnerian; here was a spirit with strange and still nameless needs, a memory bristling with questions, experiences and obscurities, beside which stood the name Dionysos like one more note of interrogation; here spoke—people said to themselves with misgivings—something like a mystic and almost mænadic soul, which, undecided whether it should disclose or conceal itself, stammers with an effort and capriciously as in a strange tongue. It should have *sung,* this "new soul"—and not spoken! What a pity, that I did not dare to say what I then had to say, as a poet: I could have done so perhaps! Or at least as a philologist:—for even at the present day well-nigh everything in this domain remains to be discovered and disinterred by the philologist! Above all the problem, *that* here there *is* a problem before us,—and that, so long as we have no answer to the question "what is Dionysian?" the Greeks are now as ever wholly unknown and inconceivable....

4.

Ay, what is Dionysian?—In this book may be found an answer,—a "knowing one" speaks here, the votary and disciple of his god. Perhaps I should now speak more guardedly and less eloquently of a psychological question so difficult as the origin of tragedy among the Greeks. A fundamental question is the relation of the Greek to pain, his degree of sensibility,—did this relation remain constant? or did it veer about?—the question, whether his ever-increasing *longing for beauty,* for festivals, gaieties, new cults, did really grow out of want, privation, melancholy, pain? For suppose even this to be true—and Pericles (or Thucydides) intimates as much in the great Funeral Speech:—whence then the opposite longing, which appeared first in the order of time, the *longing for the ugly*, the good, resolute desire of the Old Hellene for pessimism, for tragic myth, for the picture of all that is terrible, evil, enigmatical, destructive, fatal at the basis of existence,—whence then must tragedy have sprung? Perhaps from *joy,* from strength, from exuberant health, from over-fullness. And what then, physiologically speaking, is the meaning of that madness, out of which comic as well as tragic art has grown, the Dionysian madness? What? perhaps madness is not necessarily the symptom of degeneration, of decline, of belated culture? Perhaps there are—a question for alienists—neuroses of *health*? of folk-youth and youthfulness? What does that synthesis of god and goat in the Satyr point to? What self-experience what "stress," made the Greek think of the Dionysian reveller and primitive man as a satyr? And as regards the origin of the tragic chorus: perhaps there were endemic ecstasies in the eras when the Greek body bloomed and the Greek soul brimmed over with life? Visions and hallucinations, which took hold of entire communities, entire cult-assemblies? What if the Greeks in the very wealth of their youth had the will *to be* tragic and were pessimists? What if it was madness itself, to use a word of Plato's, which brought the *greatest* blessings upon Hellas? And what if, on the other hand and conversely, at the very time of their dissolution and weakness, the Greeks became always more optimistic, more superficial, more histrionic, also more ardent for logic and the logicising of the world,—consequently at the same time more "cheerful" and more "scientific"? Ay, despite all "modern ideas" and prejudices of the democratic taste, may not the triumph of *optimism,* the *common sense* that has gained the upper hand, the practical and theoretical *utilitarianism,* like democracy itself, with which it is synchronous—be symptomatic of declining vigour, of approaching age, of physiological weariness? And *not* at all—pessimism? Was Epicurus an optimist—because a *sufferer*?... We see it is a whole bundle of weighty questions which this book has taken upon itself,—let us not fail to add its weightiest question! Viewed through the optics of *life,* what is the meaning of—morality?...

5.

Already in the foreword to Richard Wagner, art—-and *not* morality—is set down as the properly *metaphysical* activity of man; in the book itself the piquant proposition recurs time and again, that the existence of the world is *justified* only as an æsthetic phenomenon. Indeed, the entire book recognises only an artist-thought and artist-after-thought behind all occurrences,—a "God," if you will, but certainly only an altogether thoughtless and unmoral artist-God, who, in construction as in destruction, in good as in evil, desires to become conscious of his own equable joy and sovereign glory; who, in creating worlds, frees himself from the *anguish* of fullness and *overfullness,* from the *suffering* of the contradictions concentrated within him. The world, that is, the redemption of God *attained* at every moment, as the perpetually changing, perpetually new vision of the most suffering, most antithetical, most contradictory being, who contrives to redeem himself only in *appearance:* this entire artist-metaphysics, call it arbitrary, idle, fantastic, if you will,—the point is, that it already betrays a spirit, which is determined some day, at all hazards, to make a stand against the *moral* interpretation and significance of life. Here, perhaps for the first time, a pessimism "Beyond Good and Evil" announces itself, here that "perverseness of disposition" obtains expression and formulation, against which Schopenhauer never grew tired of hurling beforehand his angriest imprecations and thunderbolts,—a philosophy which dares to put, derogatorily put, morality itself in the world of phenomena, and not only among "phenomena" (in the sense of the idealistic *terminus technicus*), but among the "illusions," as appearance, semblance, error, interpretation, accommodation, art. Perhaps the depth of this *antimoral* tendency may be best estimated from the guarded and hostile silence with which Christianity is treated throughout this book,—Christianity, as being the most extravagant burlesque of the moral theme to which mankind has hitherto been obliged to listen. In fact, to the purely æsthetic world-interpretation and justification taught in this book, there is no greater antithesis than the Christian dogma, which is *only* and will be only moral, and which, with its absolute standards, for instance, its truthfulness of God, relegates—that is, disowns, convicts, condemns—art, *all* art, to the realm of *falsehood.* Behind such a mode of thought and valuation, which, if at all genuine, must be hostile to art, I always experienced what was *hostile to life,* the wrathful, vindictive counterwill to life itself: for all life rests on appearance, art, illusion, optics, necessity of perspective and error. From the very first Christianity was, essentially and thoroughly, the nausea and surfeit of Life for Life, which only disguised, concealed and decked itself out under the belief in "another" or "better" life. The hatred of the "world," the curse on the affections, the fear of beauty and sensuality, another world, invented for the purpose of slandering this world the more, at bottom a longing for. Nothingness, for the end, for rest, for the "Sabbath of Sabbaths"—all this, as also the unconditional will of Christianity to recognise *only* moral values, has always appeared to me as the most dangerous and ominous of all possible forms of a "will to perish"; at the least, as the symptom of a most fatal disease, of profoundest weariness, despondency, exhaustion, impoverishment of life,—for before the tribunal of morality (especially Christian, that is, unconditional morality) life *must* constantly and inevitably be the loser, because life *is* something essentially unmoral,—indeed, oppressed with the weight of contempt and the everlasting No, life *must* finally be regarded as unworthy of desire, as in itself unworthy. Morality itself what?—may not morality be a "will to disown life," a secret instinct for annihilation, a principle of decay, of depreciation, of slander, a beginning of the end? And, consequently, the danger of dangers?... It was *against* morality, therefore, that my instinct, as an intercessory-instinct for life, turned in this questionable book, inventing for itself a fundamental counter—dogma and counter-valuation of life, purely artistic, purely *anti-Christian.* What should I call it? As a philologist and man of words I baptised it, not without some liberty—for who could be sure of the proper name of the Antichrist?—with the name of a Greek god: I called it *Dionysian.*

6.

You see which problem I ventured to touch upon in this early work?... How I now regret, that I had not then the courage (or immodesty?) to allow myself, in all respects, the use of an *individual language* for such *individual* contemplations and ventures in the field of thought—that I laboured to express, in Kantian and Schopenhauerian formulæ, strange and new valuations, which ran fundamentally counter to the spirit of Kant and Schopenhauer, as well as to their taste! What, forsooth, were Schopenhauer's views on tragedy? "What gives"—he says in *Welt als Wille und Vorstellung,* II. 495—"to all tragedy that singular swing towards elevation, is the awakening of the knowledge that the world, that life, cannot satisfy us thoroughly, and consequently is *not worthy* of our attachment In this consists the tragic spirit: it therefore leads to *resignation.*" Oh, how differently Dionysos spoke to me! Oh how far from me then was just this entire resignationism!—But there is something far worse in this book, which I now regret even more than having obscured and spoiled Dionysian anticipations with Schopenhauerian formulæ: to wit, that, in general, I *spoiled* the grand *Hellenic problem,* as it had opened up before me, by the admixture of the most modern things! That I entertained hopes, where nothing was to be hoped for, where everything pointed all-too-clearly to an approaching end! That, on the basis of our latter-day German music, I began to fable about the "spirit of Teutonism," as if it were on the point of discovering and returning to itself,—ay, at the very time that the German spirit which not so very long before had had the will to the lordship over Europe, the strength to lead and govern Europe, testamentarily and conclusively *resigned* and, under the pompous pretence of empire-founding, effected its transition to mediocritisation, democracy, and "modern ideas." In very fact, I have since learned to regard this "spirit of Teutonism" as something to be despaired of and unsparingly treated, as also our present *German music,* which is Romanticism through and through and the most un-Grecian of all possible forms of art: and moreover a first-rate nerve-destroyer, doubly dangerous for a people given to drinking and revering the unclear as a virtue, namely, in its twofold capacity of an intoxicating and stupefying narcotic. Of course, apart from all precipitate hopes and faulty applications to matters specially modern, with which I then spoiled my first book, the great Dionysian note of interrogation, as set down therein, continues standing on and on, even with reference to music: how must we conceive of a music, which is no longer of Romantic origin, like the German; but of *Dionysian*?...

7.

—But, my dear Sir, if *your* book is not Romanticism, what in the world is? Can the deep hatred of the present, of "reality" and "modern ideas" be pushed farther than has been done in your artist-metaphysics?—which would rather believe in Nothing, or in the devil, than in the "Now"? Does not a radical bass of wrath and annihilative pleasure growl on beneath all your contrapuntal vocal art and aural seduction, a mad determination to oppose all that "now" is, a will which is not so very far removed from practical nihilism and which seems to say: "rather let nothing be true, than that *you* should be in the right, than that *your* truth should prevail!" Hear, yourself, my dear Sir Pessimist and art-deifier, with ever so unlocked ears, a single select passage of your own book, that not ineloquent dragon-slayer passage, which may sound insidiously rat-charming to young ears and hearts. What? is not that the true blue romanticist-confession of 1830 under the mask of the pessimism of 1850? After which, of course, the usual romanticist finale at once strikes up,—rupture, collapse, return and prostration before an old belief, before *the* old God.... What? is not your pessimist book itself a piece of anti-Hellenism and Romanticism, something "equally intoxicating and befogging," a narcotic at all events, ay, a piece of music, of *German* music? But listen:

> Let us imagine a rising generation with this undauntedness of vision, with this heroic impulse towards the prodigious, let us imagine the bold step of these dragon-slayers, the proud daring with which they turn their backs on all the effeminate doctrines of optimism, in order "to live resolutely" in the Whole and in the Full: *would it not be necessary* for the tragic man of this culture, with his self-discipline to earnestness and terror, to desire a new art, *the art of metaphysical comfort,* tragedy as the Helena belonging to him, and that he should exclaim with Faust:
>
> "Und sollt ich nicht, sehnsüchtigster Gewalt,
> In's Leben ziehn die einzigste Gestalt?"*

"Would it not be *necessary*?" ... No, thrice no! ye young romanticists: it would *not* be necessary! But it is very probable, that things may *end* thus, that

---

* And shall not I, by mightiest desire,
In living shape that sole fair form acquire?

SWANWICK, trans. of *Faust.*

ye may end thus, namely "comforted," as it is written, in spite of all self-discipline to earnestness and terror; metaphysically comforted, in short, as Romanticists are wont to end, as *Christians*.... No! ye should first of all learn the art of earthly comfort, ye should learn to *laugh,* my young friends, if ye are at all determined to remain pessimists: if so, you will perhaps, as laughing ones, eventually send all metaphysical comfortism to the devil—and metaphysics first of all! Or, to say it in the language of that Dionysian ogre, called *Zarathustra*:

> "Lift up your hearts, my brethren, high, higher! And do not forget your legs! Lift up also your legs, ye good dancers—and better still if ye stand also on your heads!
>
> "This crown of the laughter, this rose-garland crown—I myself have put on this crown; I myself have consecrated my laughter. No one else have I found to-day strong enough for this.
>
> "Zarathustra the dancer, Zarathustra the light one, who beckoneth with his pinions, one ready for flight, beckoning unto all birds, ready and prepared, a blissfully light-spirited one:—
>
> "Zarathustra the soothsayer, Zarathustra the sooth-laugher, no impatient one, no absolute one, one who loveth leaps and side-leaps: I myself have put on this crown!
>
> "This crown of the laughter, this rose-garland crown—to you my brethren do I cast this crown! Laughing have I consecrated: ye higher men, *learn,* I pray you—to laugh!"

Thus spake Zarathustra,
lxxiii. 17, 18, and 20.

SILS-MARIA, OBERENGADIN,
August 1886.

THE BIRTH OF TRAGEDY
FROM THE SPIRIT OF MUSIC

FOREWORD TO RICHARD WAGNER

In order to keep at a distance all the possible scruples, excitements, and misunderstandings to which the thoughts gathered in this essay will give occasion, considering the peculiar character of our æsthetic publicity, and to be able also Co write the introductory remarks with the same contemplative delight, the impress of which, as the petrifaction of good and elevating hours, it bears on every page, I form a conception of the moment when you, my highly honoured friend, will receive this essay; how you, say after an evening walk in the winter snow, will behold the unbound Prometheus on the title-page, read my name, and be forthwith convinced that, whatever this essay may contain, the author has something earnest and impressive to say, and, moreover, that in all his meditations he communed with you as with one present and could thus write only what befitted your presence. You will thus remember that it was at the same time as your magnificent dissertation on Beethoven originated, viz., amidst the horrors and sublimities of the war which had just then broken out, that I collected myself for these thoughts. But those persons would err, to whom this collection suggests no more perhaps than the antithesis of patriotic excitement and æsthetic revelry, of gallant earnestness and sportive delight. Upon a real perusal of this essay, such readers will, rather to their surprise, discover how earnest is the German problem we have to deal with, which we properly place, as a vortex and turning-point, in the very midst of German hopes. Perhaps, however, this same class of readers will be shocked at seeing an æsthetic problem taken so seriously, especially if they can recognise in art no more than a merry diversion, a readily dispensable court-jester to the "earnestness of existence": as if no one were aware of the real meaning of this confrontation with the "earnestness of existence." These earnest ones may be informed that I am convinced that art is the highest task and the properly metaphysical activity of this life, as it is understood by the man, to whom, as my sublime protagonist on this path, I would now dedicate this essay.

BASEL, *end of the year* 1871.

THE BIRTH OF TRAGEDY

1.

We shall have gained much for the science of æsthetics, when once we have perceived not only by logical inference, but by the immediate certainty of intuition, that the continuous development of art is bound up with the duplexity of the *Apollonian* and the *Dionysian:* in like manner as procreation is dependent on the duality of the sexes, involving perpetual conflicts with only periodically intervening reconciliations. These names we borrow from the Greeks, who disclose to the intelligent observer the profound mysteries of their view of art, not indeed in concepts, but in the impressively clear figures of their world of deities. It is in connection with Apollo and Dionysus, the two art-deities of the Greeks, that we learn that there existed in the Grecian world a wide antithesis, in origin and aims, between the art of the shaper, the Apollonian, and the non-plastic art of music, that of Dionysus: both these so heterogeneous tendencies run parallel to each other, for the most part openly at variance, and continually inciting each other to new and more powerful births, to perpetuate in them the strife of this antithesis, which is but seemingly bridged over by their mutual term "Art"; till at last, by a metaphysical miracle of the Hellenic will, they appear paired with each other, and through this pairing eventually generate the equally Dionysian and Apollonian art-work of Attic tragedy.

In order to bring these two tendencies within closer range, let us conceive them first of all as the separate art-worlds of *dreamland* and *drunkenness;* between which physiological phenomena a contrast may be observed analogous to that existing between the Apollonian and the Dionysian. In dreams, according to the conception of Lucretius, the glorious divine figures first appeared to the souls of men, in dreams the great shaper beheld the charming corporeal structure of superhuman beings, and the Hellenic poet, if consulted on the mysteries of poetic inspiration, would likewise have suggested dreams and would have offered an explanation resembling that of Hans Sachs in the Meistersingers:—

> Mein Freund, das grad' ist Dichters Werk,
> dass er sein Träumen deut' und merk'.

Glaubt mir, des Menschen wahrster Wahn
wird ihm im Traume aufgethan:
all' Dichtkunst und Poeterei
ist nichts als Wahrtraum-Deuterei.*

The beauteous appearance of the dream-worlds, in the production of which every man is a perfect artist, is the presupposition of all plastic art, and in fact, as we shall see, of an important half of poetry also. We take delight in the immediate apprehension of form; all forms speak to us; there is nothing indifferent, nothing superfluous. But, together with the highest life of this dream-reality we also have, glimmering through it, the sensation of its appearance: such at least is my experience, as to the frequency, ay, normality of which I could adduce many proofs, as also the sayings of the poets. Indeed, the man of philosophic turn has a foreboding that underneath this reality in which we live and have our being, another and altogether different reality lies concealed, and that therefore it is also an appearance; and Schopenhauer actually designates the gift of occasionally regarding men and things as mere phantoms and dream-pictures as the criterion of philosophical ability. Accordingly, the man susceptible to art stands in the same relation to the reality of dreams as the philosopher to the reality of existence; he is a close and willing observer, for from these pictures he reads the meaning of life, and by these processes he trains himself for life. And it is perhaps not only the agreeable and friendly pictures that he realises in himself with such perfect understanding: the earnest, the troubled, the dreary, the gloomy, the sudden checks, the tricks of fortune, the uneasy presentiments, in short, the whole "Divine Comedy" of life, and the Inferno, also pass before him, not merely like pictures on the wall—for he too lives and suffers in these scenes,—and yet not without that fleeting sensation of appearance. And perhaps many a one will, like myself, recollect having sometimes called out cheeringly and not without success amid the dangers and terrors of dream-life: "It is a dream! I will dream on!" I have likewise been told of persons capable of continuing the causality of one and the same dream for three and even more successive nights: all of which facts clearly testify that our innermost being, the common substratum of all of us, experiences our dreams with deep joy and cheerful acquiescence.

This cheerful acquiescence in the dream-experience has likewise been embodied by the Greeks in their Apollo: for Apollo, as the god of all shaping

* My friend, just this is poet's task:
His dreams to read and to unmask.
Trust me, illusion's truths thrice sealed
In dream to man will be revealed.
All verse-craft and poetisation
Is but soothdream interpretation.

energies, is also the soothsaying god. He, who (as the etymology of the name indicates) is the "shining one," the deity of light, also rules over the fair appearance of the inner world of fantasies. The higher truth, the perfection of these states in contrast to the only partially intelligible everyday world, ay, the deep consciousness of nature, healing and helping in sleep and dream, is at the same time the symbolical analogue of the faculty of soothsaying and, in general, of the arts, through which life is made possible and worth living. But also that delicate line, which the dream-picture must not overstep—lest it act pathologically (in which case appearance, being reality pure and simple, would impose upon us)—must not be wanting in the picture of Apollo: that measured limitation, that freedom from the wilder emotions, that philosophical calmness of the sculptor-god. His eye must be "sunlike," according to his origin; even when it is angry and looks displeased, the sacredness of his beauteous appearance is still there. And so we might apply to Apollo, in an eccentric sense, what Schopenhauer says of the man wrapt in the veil of Mâyâ*: *Welt als Wille und Vorstellung,* I. p. 416: "Just as in a stormy sea, unbounded in every direction, rising and falling with howling mountainous waves, a sailor sits in a boat and trusts in his frail barque: so in the midst of a world of sorrows the individual sits quietly supported by and trusting in his *principium individuationis*." Indeed, we might say of Apollo, that in him the unshaken faith in this *principium* and the quiet sitting of the man wrapt therein have received their sublimest expression; and we might even designate Apollo as the glorious divine image of the *principium individuationis,* from out of the gestures and looks of which all the joy and wisdom of "appearance," together with its beauty, speak to us.

In the same work Schopenhauer has described to us the stupendous *awe* which seizes upon man, when of a sudden he is at a loss to account for the cognitive forms of a phenomenon, in that the principle of reason, in some one of its manifestations, seems to admit of an exception. Add to this awe the blissful ecstasy which rises from the innermost depths of man, ay, of nature, at this same collapse of the *principium individuationis,* and we shall gain an insight into the being of the *Dionysian,* which is brought within closest ken perhaps by the analogy of *drunkenness.* It is either under the influence of the narcotic draught, of which the hymns of all primitive men and peoples tell us, or by the powerful approach of spring penetrating all nature with joy, that those Dionysian emotions awake, in the augmentation of which the subjective vanishes to complete self-forgetfulness. So also in the German Middle Ages singing and dancing crowds, ever increasing in number, were borne from place to place under this same Dionysian power. In these St. John's and St. Vitus's dancers we again perceive the Bacchic choruses of the Greeks, with their previous history in Asia Minor, as far back as Babylon and the orgiastic Sacæa.

* Cf. *World and Will as Idea,* 1. 455 ff., trans, by Haldane and Kemp.

There are some, who, from lack of experience or obtuseness, will turn away from such phenomena as "folk-diseases" with a smile of contempt or pity prompted by the consciousness of their own health: of course, the poor wretches do not divine what a cadaverous-looking and ghastly aspect this very "health" of theirs presents when the glowing life of the Dionysian revellers rushes past them.

Under the charm of the Dionysian not only is the covenant between man and man again established, but also estranged, hostile or subjugated nature again celebrates her reconciliation with her lost son, man. Of her own accord earth proffers her gifts, and peacefully the beasts of prey approach from the desert and the rocks. The chariot of Dionysus is bedecked with flowers and garlands: panthers and tigers pass beneath his yoke. Change Beethoven's "jubilee-song" into a painting, and, if your imagination be equal to the occasion when the awestruck millions sink into the dust, you will then be able to approach the Dionysian. Now is the slave a free man, now all the stubborn, hostile barriers, which necessity, caprice, or "shameless fashion" has set up between man and man, are broken down. Now, at the evangel of cosmic harmony, each one feels himself not only united, reconciled, blended with his neighbour, but as one with him, as if the veil of Mâyâ has been torn and were now merely fluttering in tatters before the mysterious Primordial Unity. In song and in dance man exhibits himself as a member of a higher community, he has forgotten how to walk and speak, and is on the point of taking a dancing flight into the air. His gestures bespeak enchantment. Even as the animals now talk, and as the earth yields milk and honey, so also something super-natural sounds forth from him: he feels himself a god, he himself now walks about enchanted and elated even as the gods whom he saw walking about in his dreams. Man is no longer an artist, he has become a work of art: the artistic power of all nature here reveals itself in the tremors of drunkenness to the highest gratification of the Primordial Unity. The noblest clay, the costliest marble, namely man, is here kneaded and cut, and the chisel strokes of the Dionysian world-artist are accompanied with the cry of the Eleusinian mysteries: "Ihr stürzt nieder, Millionen? Ahnest du den Schöpfer, Welt?"*

2.

Thus far we have considered the Apollonian and his antithesis, the Dionysian, as artistic powers, which burst forth from nature herself, *without the mediation of the human artist,* and in which her art-impulses are satisfied in the most immediate and direct way: first, as the pictorial world of dreams,

---

* Ye bow in the dust, oh millions?
Thy maker, mortal, dost divine?
Cf. Schiller's "Hymn to Joy"; and Beethoven, Ninth Symphony.—TR.

the perfection of which has no connection whatever with the intellectual height or artistic culture of the unit man, and again, as drunken reality, which likewise does not heed the unit man, but even seeks to destroy the individual and redeem him by a mystic feeling of Oneness. Anent these immediate art-states of nature every artist is either an "imitator," to wit, either an Apollonian, an artist in dreams, or a Dionysian, an artist in ecstasies, or finally—as for instance in Greek tragedy—an artist in both dreams and ecstasies: so we may perhaps picture him, as in his Dionysian drunkenness and mystical self-abnegation, lonesome and apart from the revelling choruses, he sinks down, and how now, through Apollonian dream-inspiration, his own state, *i.e.*, his oneness with the primal source of the universe, reveals itself to him *in a symbolical dream-picture*.

After these general premisings and contrastings, let us now approach the *Greeks* in order to learn in what degree and to what height these *art-impulses of nature* were developed in them: whereby we shall be enabled to understand and appreciate more deeply the relation of the Greek artist to his archetypes, or, according to the Aristotelian expression, "the imitation of nature." In spite of all the dream-literature and the numerous dream-anecdotes of the Greeks, we can speak only conjecturally, though with a fair degree of certainty, of their *dreams*. Considering the incredibly precise and unerring plastic power of their eyes, as also their manifest and sincere delight in colours, we can hardly refrain (to the shame of every one born later) from assuming for their very dreams a logical causality of lines and contours, colours and groups, a sequence of scenes resembling their best reliefs, the perfection of which would certainly justify us, if a comparison were possible, in designating the dreaming Greeks as Homers and Homer as a dreaming Greek: in a deeper sense than when modern man, in respect to his dreams, ventures to compare himself with Shakespeare.

On the other hand, we should not have to speak conjecturally, if asked to disclose the immense gap which separated the *Dionysian Greek* from the Dionysian barbarian. From all quarters of the Ancient World—to say nothing of the modern—from Rome as far as Babylon, we can prove the existence of Dionysian festivals, the type of which bears, at best, the same relation to the Greek festivals as the bearded satyr, who borrowed his name and attributes from the goat, does to Dionysus himself. In nearly every instance the centre of these festivals lay in extravagant sexual licentiousness, the waves of which overwhelmed all family life and its venerable traditions; the very wildest beasts of nature were let loose here, including that detestable mixture of lust and cruelty which has always seemed to me the genuine "witches' draught." For some time, however, it would seem that the Greeks were perfectly secure and guarded against the feverish agitations of these festivals (—the knowledge of which entered Greece by all the channels of land and sea) by the figure of

Apollo himself rising here in full pride, who could not have held out the Gorgon's head to a more dangerous power than this grotesquely uncouth Dionysian. It is in Doric art that this majestically-rejecting attitude of Apollo perpetuated itself. This opposition became more precarious and even impossible, when, from out of the deepest root of the Hellenic nature, similar impulses finally broke forth and made way for themselves: the Delphic god, by a seasonably effected reconciliation, was now contented with taking the destructive arms from the hands of his powerful antagonist. This reconciliation marks the most important moment in the history of the Greek cult: wherever we turn our eyes we may observe the revolutions resulting from this event. It was the reconciliation of two antagonists, with the sharp demarcation of the boundary-lines to be thenceforth observed by each, and with periodical transmission of testimonials;—in reality, the chasm was not bridged over. But if we observe how, under the pressure of this conclusion of peace, the Dionysian power manifested itself, we shall now recognise in the Dionysian orgies of the Greeks, as compared with the Babylonian Sacæa and their retrogression of man to the tiger and the ape, the significance of festivals of world-redemption and days of transfiguration. Not till then does nature attain her artistic jubilee; not till then does the rupture of the *principium individuationis* become an artistic phenomenon. That horrible "witches' draught" of sensuality and cruelty was here powerless: only the curious blending and duality in the emotions of the Dionysian revellers reminds one of it—just as medicines remind one of deadly poisons,—that phenomenon, to wit, that pains beget joy, that jubilation wrings painful sounds out of the breast. From the highest joy sounds the cry of horror or the yearning wail over an irretrievable loss. In these Greek festivals a sentimental trait, as it were, breaks forth from nature, as if she must sigh over her dismemberment into individuals. The song and pantomime of such dually-minded revellers was something new and unheard-of in the Homeric-Grecian world; and the Dionysian *music* in particular excited awe and horror. If music, as it would seem, was previously known as an Apollonian art, it was, strictly speaking, only as the wave-beat of rhythm, the formative power of which was developed to the representation of Apollonian conditions. The music of Apollo was Doric architectonics in tones, but in merely suggested tones, such as those of the cithara. The very element which forms the essence of Dionysian music (and hence of music in general) is carefully excluded as un-Apollonian; namely, the thrilling power of the tone, the uniform stream of the melos, and the thoroughly incomparable world of harmony. In the Dionysian dithyramb man is incited to the highest exaltation of all his symbolic faculties; something never before experienced struggles for utterance—the annihilation of the veil of Mâyâ, Oneness as genius of the race, ay, of nature. The essence of nature is now to be expressed symbolically; a new world of symbols is required; for once the entire symbolism of the body, not only the symbolism of the lips, face, and speech, but the whole pantomime of dancing which sets all the members into rhythmical motion. Thereupon the other symbolic powers, those of music, in rhythmics, dynamics, and harmony, suddenly become impetuous. To comprehend this collective discharge of all the symbolic powers, a man must have already attained that height of self-abnegation, which wills to express itself symbolically through these powers: the Dithyrambic votary of Dionysus is therefore understood only by those like himself! With what astonishment must the Apollonian Greek have beheld him! With an astonishment, which was all the greater the more it was mingled with the shuddering suspicion that all this was in reality not so very foreign to him, yea, that, like unto a veil, his Apollonian consciousness only hid this Dionysian world from his view.

3.

In order to comprehend this, we must take down the artistic structure of the *Apollonian culture,* as it were, stone by stone, till we behold the foundations on which it rests. Here we observe first of all the glorious *Olympian* figures of the gods, standing on the gables of this structure, whose deeds, represented in far-shining reliefs, adorn its friezes. Though Apollo stands among them as an individual deity, side by side with others, and without claim to priority of rank, we must not suffer this fact to mislead us. The same impulse which embodied itself in Apollo has, in general, given birth to this whole Olympian world, and in this sense we may regard Apollo as the father thereof. What was the enormous need from which proceeded such an illustrious group of Olympian beings?

Whosoever, with another religion in his heart, approaches these Olympians and seeks among them for moral elevation, even for sanctity, for incorporeal spiritualisation, for sympathetic looks of love, will soon be obliged to turn his back on them, discouraged and disappointed. Here nothing suggests asceticism, spirituality, or duty: here only an exuberant, even triumphant life speaks to us, in which everything existing is deified, whether good or bad. And so the spectator will perhaps stand quite bewildered before this fantastic exuberance of life, and ask himself what magic potion these madly merry men could have used for enjoying life, so that, wherever they turned their eyes, Helena, the ideal image of their own existence "floating in sweet sensuality," smiled upon them. But to this spectator, already turning backwards, we must call out: "depart not hence, but hear rather what Greek folk-wisdom says of this same life, which with such inexplicable cheerfulness spreads out before thee." There is an ancient story that king Midas hunted in the forest a long time for the wise *Silenus,* the companion of Dionysus, without capturing him. When at last he fell into his hands, the king asked what was best of all and most desirable for man. Fixed and immovable, the demon remained silent, till at last, forced by the king, he broke out with shrill laughter into these words: "Oh, wretched race of a day, children of chance and misery, why do ye compel me to say to you what it were most expedient for you not to hear? What is best of all is for ever beyond your reach: not to be born, not to *be*, to be *nothing*. The second best for you, however, is soon to die."

How is the Olympian world of deities related to this folk-wisdom? Even as the rapturous vision of the tortured martyr to his sufferings.

Now the Olympian magic mountain opens, as it were, to our view and shows to us its roots. The Greek knew and felt the terrors and horrors of existence: to be able to live at all, he had to interpose the shining dream-birth of the Olympian world between himself and them. The excessive distrust of the titanic powers of nature, the Moira throning inexorably over all knowledge, the vulture of the great philanthropist Prometheus, the terrible fate of the wise Œdipus, the family curse of the Atridæ which drove Orestes to matricide; in short, that entire philosophy of the sylvan god, with its mythical exemplars, which wrought the ruin of the melancholy Etruscans—was again and again surmounted anew by the Greeks through the artistic *middle world* of the Olympians, or at least veiled and withdrawn from sight. To be able to live, the Greeks had, from direst necessity, to create these gods: which process we may perhaps picture to ourselves in this manner: that out of the original Titan thearchy of terror the Olympian thearchy of joy was evolved, by slow transitions, through the Apollonian impulse to beauty, even as roses break forth from thorny bushes. How else could this so sensitive people, so vehement in its desires, so singularly qualified for *sufferings* have endured existence, if it had not been exhibited to them in their gods, surrounded with a higher glory? The same impulse which calls art into being, as the complement and consummation of existence, seducing to a continuation of life, caused also the Olympian world to arise, in which the Hellenic "will" held up before itself a transfiguring mirror. Thus do the gods justify the life of man, in that they themselves live it—the only satisfactory Theodicy! Existence under the bright sunshine of such gods is regarded as that which is desirable in itself, and the real *grief* of the Homeric men has reference to parting from it, especially to early parting: so that we might now say of them, with a reversion of the Silenian wisdom, that "to die early is worst of all for them, the second worst is—some day to die at all." If once the lamentation is heard, it will ring out again, of the short-lived Achilles, of the leaf-like change and vicissitude of the human race, of the decay of the heroic age. It is not unworthy of the greatest hero to long for a continuation of life, ay, even as a day-labourer. So vehemently does the "will," at the Apollonian stage of development, long for this existence, so completely at one does the Homeric man feel himself with it, that the very lamentation becomes its song of praise.

Here we must observe that this harmony which is so eagerly contemplated by modern man, in fact, this oneness of man with nature, to express which

Schiller introduced the technical term "naïve," is by no means such a simple, naturally resulting and, as it were, inevitable condition, which *must* be found at the gate of every culture leading to a paradise of man: this could be believed only by an age which sought to picture to itself Rousseau's Émile also as an artist, and imagined it had found in Homer such an artist Émile, reared at Nature's bosom. Wherever we meet with the "naïve" in art, it behoves us to recognise the highest effect of the Apollonian culture, which in the first place has always to overthrow some Titanic empire and slay monsters, and which, through powerful dazzling representations and pleasurable illusions, must have triumphed over a terrible depth of world-contemplation and a most keen susceptibility to suffering. But how seldom is the naïve—that complete absorption, in the beauty of appearance—attained! And hence how inexpressibly sublime is *Homer,* who, as unit being, bears the same relation to this Apollonian folk-culture as the unit dream-artist does to the dream-faculty of the people and of Nature in general. The Homeric "naïveté" can be comprehended only as the complete triumph of the Apollonian illusion: it is the same kind of illusion as Nature so frequently employs to compass her ends. The true goal is veiled by a phantasm: we stretch out our hands for the latter, while Nature attains the former through our illusion. In the Greeks the "will" desired to contemplate itself in the transfiguration of the genius and the world of art; in order to glorify themselves, its creatures had to feel themselves worthy of glory; they had to behold themselves again in a higher sphere, without this consummate world of contemplation acting as an imperative or reproach. Such is the sphere of beauty, in which, as in a mirror, they saw their images, the Olympians. With this mirroring of beauty the Hellenic will combated its talent—correlative to the artistic—for suffering and for the wisdom of suffering: and, as a monument of its victory, Homer, the naïve artist, stands before us.

4.

Concerning this naïve artist the analogy of dreams will enlighten us to some extent. When we realise to ourselves the dreamer, as, in the midst of the illusion of the dream-world and without disturbing it, he calls out to himself: "it is a dream, I will dream on"; when we must thence infer a deep inner joy in dream-contemplation; when, on the other hand, to be at all able to dream with this inner joy in contemplation, we must have completely forgotten the day and its terrible obtrusiveness, we may, under the direction of the dream-reading Apollo, interpret all these phenomena to ourselves somewhat as follows. Though it is certain that of the two halves of life, the waking and the dreaming, the former appeals to us as by far the more preferred, important, excellent and worthy of being lived, indeed, as that which alone is lived: yet, with reference to that mysterious ground of our being of which we are the phenomenon, I should, paradoxical as it may seem, be inclined to maintain the very opposite estimate of the value of dream life. For the more clearly I perceive in nature those all-powerful art impulses, and in them a fervent longing for appearance, for redemption through appearance, the more I feel myself driven to the metaphysical assumption that the Verily-Existent and Primordial Unity, as the Eternally Suffering and Self-Contradictory, requires the rapturous vision, the joyful appearance, for its continuous salvation: which appearance we, who are completely wrapt in it and composed of it, must regard as the Verily Non-existent,—*i.e.,* as a perpetual unfolding in time, space and causality,—in other words, as empiric reality. If we therefore waive the consideration of our own "reality" for the present, if we conceive our empiric existence, and that of the world generally, as a representation of the Primordial Unity generated every moment, we shall then have to regard the dream as an *appearance of appearance,* hence as a still higher gratification of the primordial desire for appearance. It is for this same reason that the innermost heart of Nature experiences that indescribable joy in the naïve artist and in the naïve work of art, which is likewise only "an appearance of appearance." In a symbolic painting, *Raphael*, himself one of these immortal "naïve" ones, has represented to us this depotentiating of appearance to appearance, the primordial process of the naïve artist and at the same time of Apollonian culture. In his *Transfiguration,* the lower half, with the possessed boy, the despairing bearers, the helpless, terrified disciples, shows to us the reflection of eternal primordial pain, the sole basis of the world: the "appearance" here is the counter-appearance of eternal Contradiction, the father of things. Out of this appearance then arises, like an ambrosial vapour, a visionlike new world of appearances, of which those wrapt in the first appearance see nothing—a radiant floating in purest bliss and painless Contemplation beaming from wide-open eyes. Here there is presented to our view, in the highest symbolism of art, that Apollonian world of beauty and its substratum, the terrible wisdom of Silenus, and we comprehend, by intuition, their necessary interdependence. Apollo, however, again appears to us as the apotheosis of the *principium individuationis,* in which alone the perpetually attained end of the Primordial Unity, its redemption through appearance, is consummated: he shows us, with sublime attitudes, how the entire world of torment is necessary, that thereby the individual may be impelled to realise the redeeming vision, and then, sunk in contemplation thereof, quietly sit in his fluctuating barque, in the midst of the sea.

This apotheosis of individuation, if it be at all conceived as imperative and laying down precepts, knows but one law—the individual, *i.e.,* the observance of the boundaries of the individual, *measure* in the Hellenic sense. Apollo, as ethical deity, demands due proportion of his disciples, and, that this may be observed, he demands self-knowledge. And thus, parallel to the æsthetic necessity for beauty, there run the demands "know thyself" and "not too much," while presumption and undueness are regarded as the truly hostile demons of the non-Apollonian sphere, hence as characteristics of the pre-

Apollonian age, that of the Titans, and of the extra-Apollonian world, that of the barbarians. Because of his Titan-like love for man, Prometheus had to be torn to pieces by vultures; because of his excessive wisdom, which solved the riddle of the Sphinx, Œdipus had to plunge into a bewildering vortex of monstrous crimes: thus did the Delphic god interpret the Grecian past.

So also the effects wrought by the *Dionysian* appeared "titanic" and "barbaric" to the Apollonian Greek: while at the same time he could not conceal from himself that he too was inwardly related to these overthrown Titans and heroes. Indeed, he had to recognise still more than this: his entire existence, with all its beauty and moderation, rested on a hidden substratum of suffering and of knowledge, which was again disclosed to him by the Dionysian. And lo! Apollo could not live without Dionysus! The "titanic" and the "barbaric" were in the end not less necessary than the Apollonian. And now let us imagine to ourselves how the ecstatic tone of the Dionysian festival sounded in ever more luring and bewitching strains into this artificially confined world built on appearance and moderation, how in these strains all the *undueness* of nature, in joy, sorrow, and knowledge, even to the transpiercing shriek, became audible: let us ask ourselves what meaning could be attached to the psalmodising artist of Apollo, with the phantom harp-sound, as compared with this demonic folk-song! The muses of the arts of "appearance" paled before an art which, in its intoxication, spoke the truth, the wisdom of Silenus cried "woe! woe!" against the cheerful Olympians. The individual, with all his boundaries and due proportions, went under in the self-oblivion of the Dionysian states and forgot the Apollonian precepts. The *Undueness* revealed itself as truth, contradiction, the bliss born of pain, declared itself but of the heart of nature. And thus, wherever the Dionysian prevailed, the Apollonian was routed and annihilated. But it is quite as certain that, where the first assault was successfully withstood, the authority and majesty of the Delphic god exhibited itself as more rigid and menacing than ever. For I can only explain to myself the *Doric* state and Doric art as a permanent war-camp of the Apollonian: only by incessant opposition to the titanic-barbaric nature of the Dionysian was it possible for an art so defiantly-prim, so encompassed with bulwarks, a training so warlike and rigorous, a constitution so cruel and relentless, to last for any length of time.

Up to this point we have enlarged upon the observation made at the beginning of this essay: how the Dionysian and the Apollonian, in ever new births succeeding and mutually augmenting one another, controlled the Hellenic genius: how from out the age of "bronze," with its Titan struggles and rigorous folk-philosophy, the Homeric world develops under the fostering sway of the Apollonian impulse to beauty, how this "naïve" splendour is again overwhelmed by the inbursting flood of the Dionysian, and how against this new power the Apollonian rises to the austere majesty of Doric art and the Doric view of things. If, then, in this way, in the strife of these two hostile principles, the older Hellenic history falls into four great periods of art, we are now driven to inquire after the ulterior purpose of these unfoldings and processes, unless perchance we should regard the last-attained period, the period of Doric art, as the end and aim of these artistic impulses: and here the sublime and highly celebrated art-work of *Attic tragedy* and dramatic dithyramb presents itself to our view as the common goal of both these impulses, whose mysterious union, after many and long precursory struggles, found its glorious consummation in such a child,—which is at once Antigone and Cassandra.

5.

We now approach the real purpose of our investigation, which aims at acquiring a knowledge of the Dionyso-Apollonian genius and his art-work, or at least an anticipatory understanding of the mystery of the aforesaid union. Here we shall ask first of all where that new germ which subsequently developed into tragedy and dramatic dithyramb first makes itself perceptible in the Hellenic world. The ancients themselves supply the answer in symbolic form, when they place *Homer* and *Archilochus* as the forefathers and torch-bearers of Greek poetry side by side on gems, sculptures, etc., in the sure conviction that only these two thoroughly original compeers, from whom a stream of fire flows over the whole of Greek posterity, should be taken into consideration. Homer, the aged dreamer sunk in himself, the type of the Apollonian naïve artist, beholds now with astonishment the impassioned genius of the warlike votary of the muses, Archilochus, violently tossed to and fro on the billows of existence: and modern æsthetics could only add by way of interpretation, that here the "objective" artist is confronted by the first "subjective" artist. But this interpretation is of little service to us, because we know the subjective artist only as the poor artist, and in every type and elevation of art we demand specially and first of all the conquest of the Subjective, the redemption from the "ego" and the cessation of every individual will and desire; indeed, we find it impossible to believe in any truly artistic production, however insignificant, without objectivity, without pure, interestless contemplation. Hence our æsthetics must first solve the problem as to how the "lyrist" is possible as an artist: he who according to the experience of all ages continually says "I" and sings off to us the entire chromatic scale of his passions and desires. This very Archilochus appals us, alongside of Homer, by his cries of hatred and scorn, by the drunken outbursts of his desire. Is not just he then, who has been called the first subjective artist, the non-artist proper? But whence then the reverence which was shown to him—the poet—in very remarkable utterances by the Delphic oracle itself, the focus of "objective" art?

Schiller has enlightened us concerning his poetic procedure by a psychological observation, inexplicable to himself, yet not apparently open to any objection. He acknowledges that as the preparatory state to the act of poetising he had not perhaps before him or within him a series of pictures with co-ordinate causality of thoughts, but rather a *musical mood* ("The perception with me is at first without a clear and definite object; this forms itself later. A certain musical mood of mind precedes, and only after this does the poetical idea follow with me.") Add to this the most important phenomenon of all ancient lyric poetry, *the union,* regarded everywhere as natural, *of the lyrist with the musician,* their very identity, indeed,—compared with which our modern lyric poetry is like the statue of a god without a head,—and we may now, on the basis of our metaphysics of æsthetics set forth above, interpret the lyrist to ourselves as follows. As Dionysian artist he is in the first place become altogether one with the Primordial Unity, its pain and contradiction, and he produces the copy of this Primordial Unity as music, granting that music has been correctly termed a repetition and a recast of the world; but now, under the Apollonian dream-inspiration, this music again becomes visible to him as in a *symbolic dream-picture.* The formless and intangible reflection of the primordial pain in music, with its redemption in appearance, then generates a second mirroring as a concrete symbol or example. The artist has already surrendered his subjectivity in the Dionysian process: the picture which now shows to him his oneness with the heart of the world, is a dream-scene, which embodies the primordial contradiction and primordial pain, together with the primordial joy, of appearance. The "I" of the lyrist sounds therefore from the abyss of being: its "subjectivity," in the sense of the modern æsthetes, is a fiction. When Archilochus, the first lyrist of the Greeks, makes known both his mad love and his contempt to the daughters of Lycambes, it is not his passion which dances before us in orgiastic frenzy: we see Dionysus and the Mænads, we see the drunken reveller Archilochus sunk down to sleep—as Euripides depicts it in the Bacchæ, the sleep on the high Alpine pasture, in the noonday sun:—and now Apollo approaches and touches him with the laurel. The Dionyso-musical enchantment of the sleeper now emits, as it were, picture sparks, lyrical poems, which in their highest development are called tragedies and dramatic dithyrambs.

The plastic artist, as also the epic poet, who is related to him, is sunk in the pure contemplation of pictures. The Dionysian musician is, without any picture, himself just primordial pain and the primordial re-echoing thereof. The lyric genius is conscious of a world of pictures and symbols—growing out of the state of mystical self-abnegation and oneness,—which has a colouring causality and velocity quite different from that of the world of the plastic artist and epic poet. While the latter lives in these pictures, and only in them, with joyful satisfaction, and never grows tired of contemplating them with love, even in their minutest characters, while even the picture of the angry Achilles is to him but a picture, the angry expression of which he enjoys with the dream-joy in appearance—so that, by this mirror of appearance, he is guarded against being unified and blending with his figures;—the pictures of the lyrist on the other hand are nothing but *his very* self and, as it were, only different projections of himself, on account of which he as the moving centre of this world is entitled to say "I": only of course this self is not the same as that of the waking, empirically real man, but the only verily existent and eternal self resting at the basis of things, by means of the images whereof the lyric genius sees through even to this basis of things. Now let us suppose that he beholds *himself* also among these images as non-genius, *i.e.,* his subject, the whole throng of subjective passions and impulses of the will directed to a definite object which appears real to him; if now it seems as if the lyric genius and the allied non-genius were one, and as if the former spoke that little word "I" of his own accord, this appearance will no longer be able to lead us astray, as it certainly led those astray who designated the lyrist as the subjective poet. In truth, Archilochus, the passionately inflamed, loving and hating man, is but a vision of the genius, who by this time is no longer Archilochus, but a genius of the world, who expresses his primordial pain symbolically in the figure of the man Archilochus: while the subjectively willing and desiring man, Archilochus, can never at any time be a poet. It is by no means necessary, however, that the lyrist should see nothing but the phenomenon of the man Archilochus before him as a reflection of eternal being; and tragedy shows how far the visionary world of the lyrist may depart from this phenomenon, to which, of course, it is most intimately related.

Schopenhauer, who did not shut his eyes to the difficulty presented by the lyrist in the philosophical contemplation of art, thought he had found a way out of it, on which, however, I cannot accompany him; while he alone, in his profound metaphysics of music, held in his hands the means whereby this difficulty could be definitely removed: as I believe I have removed it here in his spirit and to his honour. In contrast to our view, he describes the peculiar nature of song as follows* (*Welt als Wille und Vorstellung,* I. 295):—"It is the subject of the will, *i.e.,* his own volition, which fills the consciousness of the singer; often as an unbound and satisfied desire (joy), but still more often as a restricted desire (grief), always as an emotion, a passion, or an agitated frame of mind. Besides this, however, and along with it, by the sight of surrounding nature, the singer becomes conscious of himself as the subject of pure will-less knowing, the unbroken, blissful peace of which now appears, in contrast to the stress of desire, which is always restricted and always needy. The feeling of this contrast, this alternation, is really what the song as a whole expresses and what principally constitutes the lyrical state of mind. In it pure knowing comes to us as it were to deliver us from desire and the stress thereof: we

* *World as Will and Idea,* I. 323, 4th ed. of Haldane and Kemp's translation. Quoted with a few changes.

follow, but only for an instant; for desire, the remembrance of our personal ends, tears us anew from peaceful contemplation; yet ever again the next beautiful surrounding in which the pure will-less knowledge presents itself to us, allures us away from desire. Therefore, in song and in the lyrical mood, desire (the personal interest of the ends) and the pure perception of the surrounding which presents itself, are wonderfully mingled with each other; connections between them are sought for and imagined; the subjective disposition, the affection of the will, imparts its own hue to the contemplated surrounding, and conversely, the surroundings communicate the reflex of their colour to the will. The true song is the expression of the whole of this mingled and divided state of mind."

Who could fail to see in this description that lyric poetry is here characterised as an imperfectly attained art, which seldom and only as it were in leaps arrives at its goal, indeed, as a semi-art, the essence of which is said to consist in this, that desire and pure contemplation, *i.e.,* the unæsthetic and the æsthetic condition, are wonderfully mingled with each other? We maintain rather, that this entire antithesis, according to which, as according to some standard of value, Schopenhauer, too, still classifies the arts, the antithesis between the subjective and the objective, is quite out of place in æsthetics, inasmuch as the subject *i.e.,* the desiring individual who furthers his own egoistic ends, can be conceived only as the adversary, not as the origin of art. In so far as the subject is the artist, however, he has already been released from his individual will, and has become as it were the medium, through which the one verily existent Subject celebrates his redemption in appearance. For this one thing must above all be clear to us, to our humiliation *and* exaltation, that the entire comedy of art is not at all performed, say, for our betterment and culture, and that we are just as little the true authors of this art-world: rather we may assume with regard to ourselves, that its true author uses us as pictures and artistic projections, and that we have our highest dignity in our significance as works of art—for only as an *æsthetic phenomenon* is existence and the world eternally *justified:*—while of course our consciousness of this our specific significance hardly differs from the kind of consciousness which the soldiers painted on canvas have of the battle represented thereon. Hence all our knowledge of art is at bottom quite illusory, because, as knowing persons we are not one and identical with the Being who, as the sole author and spectator of this comedy of art, prepares a perpetual entertainment for himself. Only in so far as the genius in the act of artistic production coalesces with this primordial artist of the world, does he get a glimpse of the eternal essence of art, for in this state he is, in a marvellous manner, like the weird picture of the fairy-tale which can at will turn its eyes and behold itself; he is now at once subject and object, at once poet, actor, and spectator.

6.

With reference to Archilochus, it has been established by critical research that he introduced the *folk-song* into literature, and, on account thereof, deserved, according to the general estimate of the Greeks, his unique position alongside of Homer. But what is this popular folk-song in contrast to the wholly Apollonian epos? What else but the *perpetuum vestigium* of a union of the Apollonian and the Dionysian? Its enormous diffusion among all peoples, still further enhanced by ever new births, testifies to the power of this artistic double impulse of nature: which leaves its vestiges in the popular song in like manner as the orgiastic movements of a people perpetuate themselves in its music. Indeed, one might also furnish historical proofs, that every period which is highly productive in popular songs has been most violently stirred by Dionysian currents, which we must always regard as the substratum and prerequisite of the popular song.

First of all, however, we regard the popular song as the musical mirror of the world, as the Original melody, which now seeks for itself a parallel dream-phenomenon and expresses it in poetry. *Melody is therefore primary and universal,* and as such may admit of several objectivations, in several texts. Likewise, in the naïve estimation of the people, it is regarded as by far the more important and necessary. Melody generates the poem out of itself by an ever-recurring process. *The strophic form of the popular song* points to the same phenomenon, which I always beheld with astonishment, till at last I found this explanation. Any one who in accordance with this theory examines a collection of popular songs, such as "Des Knaben Wunderhorn," will find innumerable instances of the perpetually productive melody scattering picture sparks all around: which in their variegation, their abrupt change, their mad precipitance, manifest a power quite unknown to the epic appearance and its steady flow. From the point of view of the epos, this unequal and irregular pictorial world of lyric poetry must be simply condemned: and the solemn epic rhapsodists of the Apollonian festivals in the age of Terpander have certainly done so.

Accordingly, we observe that in the poetising of the popular song, language is strained to its utmost *to imitate music;* and hence a new world of poetry begins with Archilochus, which is fundamentally opposed to the Homeric. And in saying this we have pointed out the only possible relation between poetry and music, between word and tone: the word, the picture, the concept here seeks an expression analogous to music and now experiences in itself the power of music. In this sense we may discriminate between two main currents in the history of the language of the Greek people, according as their language imitated either the world of phenomena and of pictures, or the world of music. One has only to reflect seriously on the linguistic difference with regard to colour, syntactical structure, and vocabulary in Homer and Pindar, in order to comprehend the significance of this contrast; indeed, it becomes palpably clear to us that in the period between Homer and Pindar the *orgiastic flute tones of Olympus* must have sounded forth, which, in an age as late as Aristotle's, when music was infinitely more developed, transported people to drunken enthusiasm, and which, when their influence was first felt, undoubtedly incited all the poetic means of expression of contemporaneous man to imitation. I here call attention to a familiar phenomenon of our own times, against which our æsthetics raises many objections. We again and again have occasion to observe how a symphony of Beethoven compels the individual hearers to use figurative speech, though the appearance presented by a collocation of the different pictorial world generated by a piece of music may be never so fantastically diversified and even contradictory. To practise its small wit on such compositions, and to overlook a phenomenon which is certainly worth explaining, is quite in keeping with this æsthetics. Indeed, even if the tone-poet has spoken in pictures concerning a composition, when for instance he designates a certain symphony as the "pastoral" symphony, or a passage therein as "the scene by the brook," or another as the "merry gathering of rustics," these are likewise only symbolical representations born out of music—and not perhaps the imitated objects of music—representations which can give us no information whatever concerning the *Dionysian* content of music, and which in fact have no distinctive value of their own alongside of other pictorical expressions. This process of a discharge of music in pictures we have now to transfer to some youthful, linguistically productive people, to get a notion as to how the strophic popular song originates, and how the entire faculty of speech is stimulated by this new principle of imitation of music.

If, therefore, we may regard lyric poetry as the effulguration of music in pictures and concepts, we can now ask: "how does music *appear* in the mirror of symbolism and conception?" *It appears as will,* taking the word in the Schopenhauerian sense, *i.e.,* as the antithesis of the æsthetic, purely contemplative, and passive frame of mind. Here, however, we must discriminate as sharply as possible between the concept of essentiality and the concept of phenominality; for music, according to its essence, cannot be will, because as such it would have to be wholly banished from the domain of art—for the will is the unæsthetic-in-itself;—yet it appears as will. For in order to express the phenomenon of music in pictures, the lyrist requires all the stirrings of passion, from the whispering of infant desire to the roaring of madness. Under the impulse to speak of music in Apollonian symbols, he conceives of all nature, and himself therein, only as the eternally willing, desiring, longing existence. But in so far as he interprets music by means of pictures, he himself rests in the quiet calm of Apollonian contemplation, however much all around him which he beholds through the medium of music is in a state of confused and violent motion. Indeed, when he beholds himself through this same medium, his own image appears to him in a state of unsatisfied feeling: his own willing, longing, moaning and rejoicing are to him symbols by which he interprets music. Such is the phenomenon of the lyrist: as Apollonian genius he interprets music through the image of the will, while he himself, completely released from the avidity of the will, is the pure, undimmed eye of day.

Our whole disquisition insists on this, that lyric poetry is dependent on the spirit of music just as music itself in its absolute sovereignty does not *require* the picture and the concept, but only *endures* them as accompaniments. The poems of the lyrist can express nothing which has not already been contained in the vast universality and absoluteness of the music which compelled him to use figurative speech. By no means is it possible for language adequately to render the cosmic symbolism of music, for the very reason that music stands in symbolic relation to the primordial contradiction and primordial pain in the heart of the Primordial Unity, and therefore symbolises a sphere which is above all appearance and before all phenomena. Rather should we say that all phenomena, compared with it, are but symbols: hence *language*, as the organ and symbol of phenomena, cannot at all disclose the innermost essence, of music; language can only be in superficial contact with music when it attempts to imitate music; while the profoundest significance of the latter cannot be brought one step nearer to us by all the eloquence of lyric poetry.

7.

We shall now have to avail ourselves of all the principles of art hitherto considered, in order to find our way through the labyrinth, as we must designate *the origin of Greek tragedy.* I shall not be charged with absurdity in saying that the problem of this origin has as yet not even been seriously stated, not to say solved, however often the fluttering tatters of ancient tradition have been sewed together in sundry combinations and torn asunder again. This tradition tells us in the most unequivocal terms, *that tragedy sprang from the tragic chorus,* and was originally only chorus and nothing but chorus: and hence we feel it our duty to look into the heart of this tragic chorus as being the real proto-drama, without in the least contenting ourselves with current art-phraseology—according to which the chorus is the ideal spectator, or represents the people in contrast to the regal side of the scene. The latter explanatory notion, which sounds sublime to many a politician—that the immutable moral law was embodied by the democratic Athenians in the popular chorus, which always carries its point over the passionate excesses and extravagances of kings—may be ever so forcibly suggested by an observation of Aristotle: still it has no bearing on the original formation of tragedy, inasmuch as the entire antithesis of king and people, and, in general, the whole politico-social sphere, is excluded from the purely religious beginnings of tragedy; but, considering the well-known classical form of the chorus in Æschylus and Sophocles, we should even deem it blasphemy to speak here of the anticipation of a "constitutional representation of the people," from which blasphemy others have not shrunk, however. The ancient governments knew of no constitutional representation of the people *in praxi,* and it is to be hoped that they did not even so much as "anticipate" it in tragedy.

Much more celebrated than this political explanation of the chorus is the notion of A. W. Schlegel, who advises us to regard the chorus, in a manner, as the essence and extract of the crowd of spectators,—as the "ideal spectator." This view when compared with the historical tradition that tragedy was originally only chorus, reveals itself in its true character, as a crude, unscientific, yet brilliant assertion, which, however, has acquired its brilliancy only through its concentrated form of expression, through the truly Germanic bias in favour of whatever is called "ideal," and through our momentary astonishment. For we are indeed astonished the moment we compare our well-known theatrical public with this chorus, and ask ourselves if it could ever be possible to idealise something analogous to the Greek chorus out of such a public. We tacitly deny this, and now wonder as much at the boldness of Schlegel's assertion as at the totally different nature of the Greek public. For hitherto we always believed that the true spectator, be he who he may, had always to remain conscious of having before him a work of art, and not an empiric reality: whereas the tragic chorus of the Greeks is compelled to recognise real beings in the figures of the stage. The chorus of the Oceanides really believes that it sees before it the Titan Prometheus, and considers itself as real as the god of the scene. And are we to own that he is the highest and purest type of spectator, who, like the Oceanides, regards Prometheus as real and present in body? And is it characteristic of the ideal spectator that he should run on the stage and free the god from his torments? We had believed in an æsthetic public, and considered the individual spectator the better qualified the more he was capable of viewing a work of art as art, that is, æsthetically; but now the Schlegelian expression has intimated to us, that the perfect ideal spectator does not at all suffer the world of the scenes to act æsthetically on him, but corporeo-empirically. Oh, these Greeks! we have sighed; they will upset our æsthetics! But once accustomed to it, we have reiterated the saying of Schlegel, as often as the subject of the chorus has been broached.

But the tradition which is so explicit here speaks against Schlegel: the chorus as such, without the stage,—the primitive form of tragedy,—and the chorus of ideal spectators do not harmonise. What kind of art would that be which was extracted from the concept of the spectator, and whereof we are to regard the "spectator as such" as the true form? The spectator without the play is something absurd. We fear that the birth of tragedy can be explained neither by the high esteem for the moral intelligence of the multitude nor by the concept of the spectator without the play; and we regard the problem as too deep to be even so much as touched by such superficial modes of contemplation.

An infinitely more valuable insight into the signification of the chorus had already been displayed by Schiller in the celebrated Preface to his Bride of Messina, where he regarded the chorus as a living wall which tragedy draws round herself to guard her from contact with the world of reality, and to preserve her ideal domain and poetical freedom.

It is with this, his chief weapon, that Schiller combats the ordinary conception of the natural, the illusion ordinarily required in dramatic poetry. He contends that while indeed the day on the stage is merely artificial, the architecture only symbolical, and the metrical dialogue purely ideal in character, nevertheless an erroneous view still prevails in the main: that it is not enough to tolerate merely as a poetical license *that* which is in reality the essence of all poetry. The introduction of the chorus is, he says, the decisive step by which war is declared openly and honestly against all naturalism in art.—It is, methinks, for disparaging this mode of contemplation that our would-be superior age has coined the disdainful catchword "pseudo-idealism." I fear, however, that we on the other hand with our present worship of the natural and the real have landed at the nadir of all idealism, namely in the region of cabinets of wax-figures. An art indeed exists also here, as in certain novels much in vogue at present: but let no one pester us with the claim that by this art the Schiller-Goethian "Pseudo-idealism" has been vanquished.

It is indeed an "ideal" domain, as Schiller rightly perceived, upon—which the Greek satyric chorus, the chorus of primitive tragedy, was wont to walk, a domain raised far above the actual path of mortals. The Greek framed for this chorus the suspended scaffolding of a fictitious *natural state* and placed thereon fictitious *natural beings*. It is on this foundation that tragedy grew up, and so it could of course dispense from the very first with a painful portrayal of reality. Yet it is, not an arbitrary world placed by fancy betwixt heaven and earth; rather is it a world possessing the same reality and trustworthiness that Olympus with its dwellers possessed for the believing Hellene. The satyr, as being the Dionysian chorist, lives in a religiously acknowledged reality under the sanction of the myth and cult. That tragedy begins with him, that the Dionysian wisdom of tragedy speaks through him, is just as surprising a phenomenon to us as, in general, the derivation of tragedy from the chorus. Perhaps we shall get a starting-point for our inquiry, if I put forward the proposition that the satyr, the fictitious natural being, is to the man of culture what Dionysian music is to civilisation. Concerning this latter, Richard Wagner says that it is neutralised by music even as lamplight by daylight. In like manner, I believe, the Greek man of culture felt himself neutralised in the presence of the satyric chorus: and this is the most immediate effect of the Dionysian tragedy, that the state and society, and, in general, the gaps between man and man give way to an overwhelming feeling of oneness, which leads back to the heart of nature. The metaphysical comfort,—with which, as I have here intimated, every true tragedy dismisses us—that, in spite of the perpetual change of phenomena, life at bottom is indestructibly powerful and pleasurable, this comfort appears with corporeal lucidity as the satyric chorus, as the chorus of natural beings, who live ineradicable as it were behind all civilisation, and who, in spite of the ceaseless change of generations and the history of nations, remain for ever the same.

With this chorus the deep-minded Hellene, who is so singularly qualified for the most delicate and severe suffering, consoles himself:—he who has glanced with piercing eye into the very heart of the terrible destructive processes of so-called universal history, as also into the cruelty of nature, and is in danger of longing for a Buddhistic negation of the will. Art saves him, and through art life saves him—for herself.

For we must know that in the rapture of the Dionysian state, with its annihilation of the ordinary bounds and limits of existence, there is a *lethargic* element, wherein all personal experiences of the past are submerged. It is by this gulf of oblivion that the everyday world and the world of Dionysian reality are separated from each other. But as soon as this everyday reality rises again in consciousness, it is felt as such, and nauseates us; an ascetic will-paralysing mood is the fruit of these states. In this sense the Dionysian man may be said to resemble Hamlet: both have for once seen into the true nature of things, —they have *perceived,* but they are loath to act; for their action cannot change the eternal nature of things; they regard it as shameful or ridiculous that one should require of them to set aright the time which is out of joint. Knowledge kills action, action requires the veil of illusion—it is this lesson which Hamlet teaches, and not the cheap wisdom of John-a-Dreams who from too much reflection, as it were from a surplus of possibilities, does not arrive at action at all. Not reflection, no!—true knowledge, insight into appalling truth, preponderates over all motives inciting to action, in Hamlet as well as in the Dionysian man. No comfort avails any longer; his longing goes beyond a world after death, beyond the gods themselves; existence with its glittering reflection in the gods, or in an immortal other world is abjured. In the consciousness of the truth he has perceived, man now sees everywhere only the awfulness or the absurdity of existence, he now understands the symbolism in the fate of Ophelia, he now discerns the wisdom of the sylvan god Silenus: and loathing seizes him.

Here, in this extremest danger of the will, *art* approaches, as a saving and healing enchantress; she alone is able to transform these nauseating reflections on the awfulness or absurdity of existence into representations wherewith it is possible to live: these are the representations of the *sublime* as the artistic subjugation of the awful, and the *comic* as the artistic delivery from the nausea of the absurd. The satyric chorus of dithyramb is the saving deed of Greek art; the paroxysms described above spent their force in the intermediary world of these Dionysian followers.

8.

The satyr, like the idyllic shepherd of our more recent time, is the offspring of a longing after the Primitive and the Natural; but mark with what firmness and fearlessness the Greek embraced the man of the woods, and again, how coyly and mawkishly the modern man dallied with the flattering picture of a tender, flute-playing, soft-natured shepherd! Nature, on which as yet no knowledge has been at work, which maintains unbroken barriers to culture—this is what the Greek saw in his satyr, which still was not on this account supposed to coincide with the ape. On the contrary: it was the archetype of man, the embodiment of his highest and strongest emotions, as the enthusiastic reveller enraptured By the proximity of his god, as the fellow-suffering companion in whom the suffering of the god repeats itself, as the herald of wisdom speaking from the very depths of nature, as the emblem of the sexual omnipotence of nature, which the Greek was wont to contemplate with reverential awe. The satyr was something sublime and godlike: he could not but appear so, especially to the sad and wearied eye of the Dionysian man. He would have been offended by our spurious tricked-up shepherd, while his eye dwelt with sublime satisfaction on the naked and unstuntedly magnificent characters of nature: here the illusion of culture was brushed away from the archetype of man; here the true man, the bearded satyr, revealed himself, who shouts joyfully to his god. Before him the cultured man shrank to a lying caricature. Schiller is right also with reference to these beginnings of tragic art: the chorus is a living bulwark against the onsets of reality, because it—the satyric chorus—portrays existence more truthfully, more realistically, more perfectly than the cultured man who ordinarily considers himself as the only reality. The sphere of poetry does not lie outside the world, like some fantastic impossibility of a poet's imagination: it seeks to be the very opposite, the unvarnished expression of truth, and must for this very reason cast aside the false finery of that supposed reality of the cultured man. The contrast between this intrinsic truth of nature and the falsehood of culture, which poses as the only reality, is similar to that existing between the eternal kernel of things, the thing in itself, and the collective world of phenomena. And even as tragedy, with its metaphysical comfort, points to the eternal life of this kernel of existence, notwithstanding the perpetual dissolution of phenomena, so the symbolism of the satyric chorus already expresses figuratively this primordial relation between the thing in itself and phenomenon. The idyllic shepherd of the modern man is but a copy of the sum of the illusions of culture which he calls nature; the Dionysian Greek desires truth and nature in their most potent form;—he sees himself metamorphosed into the satyr.

The revelling crowd of the votaries of Dionysus rejoices, swayed by such moods and perceptions, the power of which transforms them before their own eyes, so that they imagine they behold themselves as reconstituted genii of nature, as satyrs. The later constitution of the tragic chorus is the artistic imitation of this natural phenomenon, which of course required a separation of the Dionysian spectators from the enchanted Dionysians. However, we must never lose sight of the fact that the public of the Attic tragedy rediscovered itself in the chorus of the orchestra, that there was in reality no antithesis of public and chorus: for all was but one great sublime chorus of dancing and singing satyrs, or of such as allowed themselves to be represented by the satyrs. The Schlegelian observation must here reveal itself to us in a deeper sense. The chorus is the "ideal spectator"* in so far as it is the only *beholder,*† the beholder of the visionary world of the scene. A public of spectators, as known to us, was unknown to the Greeks. In their theatres the terraced structure of the spectators' space rising in concentric arcs enabled every one, in the strictest sense, to *overlook* the entire world of culture around him, and in surfeited contemplation to imagine himself a chorist. According to this view, then, we may call the chorus in its primitive stage in proto-tragedy, a self-mirroring of the Dionysian man: a phenomenon which may be best exemplified by the process of the actor, who, if he be truly gifted, sees hovering before his eyes with almost tangible perceptibility the character he is to represent. The satyric chorus is first of all a vision of the Dionysian throng, just as the world of the stage is, in turn, a vision of the satyric chorus: the power of this vision is great enough to render the eye dull and insensible to the impression of "reality," to the presence of the cultured men occupying the tiers of seats on every side. The form of the Greek theatre reminds one of a lonesome mountain-valley: the architecture of the scene appears like a luminous cloud-picture which the Bacchants swarming on the mountains behold from the heights, as the splendid encirclement in the midst of which the image of Dionysus is revealed to them.

Owing to our learned conception of the elementary artistic processes, this artistic proto-phenomenon, which is here introduced to explain the tragic chorus, is almost shocking: while nothing can be more certain than that the poet is a poet only in that he beholds himself surrounded by forms which live and act before him, into the innermost being of which his glance penetrates. By reason of a strange defeat in our capacities, we modern men are apt to represent to ourselves the æsthetic proto-phenomenon as too complex and abstract. For the true poet the metaphor is not a rhetorical figure, but a vicarious image which actually hovers before him in place of a concept. The character

* Zuschauer.

† Schauer.

is not for him an aggregate composed of a studied collection of particular traits, but an irrepressibly live person appearing before his eyes, and differing only from the corresponding vision of the painter by its ever continued life and action. Why is it that Homer sketches much more vividly* than all the other poets? Because he contemplates† much more. We talk so abstractly about poetry, because we are all wont to be bad poets. At bottom the æsthetic phenomenon is simple: let a man but have the faculty of perpetually seeing a lively play and of constantly living surrounded by hosts of spirits, then he is a poet: let him but feel the impulse to transform himself and to talk from out the bodies and souls of others, then he is a dramatist.

The Dionysian excitement is able to impart to a whole mass of men this artistic faculty of seeing themselves surrounded by such a host of spirits, with whom they know themselves to be inwardly one. This function of the tragic chorus is the *dramatic* proto-phenomenon: to see one's self transformed before one's self, and then to act as if one had really entered into another body, into another character. This function stands at the beginning of the development of the drama. Here we have something different from the rhapsodist, who does not blend with his pictures, but only sees them, like the painter, with contemplative eye outside of him; here we actually have a surrender of the individual by his entering into another nature. Moreover this phenomenon appears in the form of an epidemic: a whole throng feels itself metamorphosed in this wise. Hence it is that the dithyramb is essentially different from every other variety of the choric song. The virgins, who with laurel twigs in their hands solemnly proceed to the temple of Apollo and sing a processional hymn, remain what they are and retain their civic names: the dithyrambic chorus is a chorus of transformed beings, whose civic past and social rank are totally forgotten: they have become the timeless servants of their god that live aloof from all the spheres of society. Every other variety of the choric lyric of the Hellenes is but an enormous enhancement of the Apollonian unit-singer: while in the dithyramb we have before us a community of unconscious actors, who mutually regard themselves as transformed among one another.

This enchantment is the prerequisite of all dramatic art. In this enchantment the Dionysian reveller sees himself as a satyr, *and as satyr he in turn beholds the god,* that is, in his transformation he sees a new vision outside him as the Apollonian consummation of his state. With this new vision the drama is complete.

According to this view, we must understand Greek tragedy as the Dionysian chorus, which always disburdens itself anew in an Apollonian world of pictures. The choric parts, therefore, with which tragedy is interlaced, are in a manner

* Anschaulicher.

† Anschaut.

the mother-womb of the entire so-called dialogue, that is, of the whole stage-world, of the drama proper. In several successive outbursts does this primordial basis of tragedy beam forth the vision of the drama, which is a dream-phenomenon throughout, and, as such, epic in character: on the other hand, however, as objectivation of a Dionysian state, it does not represent the Apollonian redemption in appearance, but, conversely, the dissolution of the individual and his unification with primordial existence. Accordingly, the drama is the Apollonian embodiment of Dionysian perceptions and influences, and is thereby separated from the epic as by an immense gap.

The *chorus* of Greek tragedy, the symbol of the mass of the people moved by Dionysian excitement, is thus fully explained by our conception of it as here set forth. Whereas, being accustomed to the position of a chorus on the modern stage, especially an operatic chorus, we could never comprehend why the tragic chorus of the Greeks should be older, more primitive, indeed, more important than the "action" proper,—as has been so plainly declared by the voice of tradition; whereas, furthermore, we could not reconcile with this traditional paramount importance and primitiveness the fact of the chorus' being composed only of humble, ministering beings; indeed, at first only of goatlike satyrs; whereas, finally, the orchestra before the scene was always a riddle to us; we have learned to comprehend at length that the scene, together with the action, was fundamentally and originally conceived only as a *vision,* that the only reality is just the chorus, which of itself generates the vision and speaks thereof with the entire symbolism of dancing, tone, and word. This chorus beholds in the vision its lord and master Dionysus, and is thus for ever the *serving* chorus: it sees how he, the god, suffers and glorifies himself, and therefore does not itself *act.* But though its attitude towards the god is throughout the attitude of ministration, this is nevertheless the highest expression, the Dionysian expression of *Nature,* and therefore, like Nature herself, the chorus utters oracles and wise sayings when transported with enthusiasm: as *fellow-sufferer* it is also the *sage* proclaiming truth from out the heart of Nature. Thus, then, originates the fantastic figure, which seems so shocking, of the wise and enthusiastic satyr, who is at the same time "the dumb man" in contrast to the god: the image of Nature and her strongest impulses, yea, the symbol of Nature, and at the same time the herald of her art and wisdom: musician, poet, dancer, and visionary in one person.

Agreeably to this view, and agreeably to tradition, *Dionysus,* the proper stage-hero and focus of vision, is not at first actually present in the oldest period of tragedy, but is only imagined as present: *i.e.,* tragedy is originally only "chorus" and not "drama." Later on the attempt is made to exhibit the god as real and to display the visionary figure together with its glorifying encirclement before the eyes of all; it is here that the "drama" in the narrow sense of the term begins. To the dithyrambic chorus is now assigned the task of exciting the minds of the hearers to such a pitch of Dionysian frenzy, that, when the tragic hero appears on the stage, they do not behold in him, say, the unshapely masked man, but a visionary figure, born as it were of their own ecstasy. Let us picture Admetes thinking in profound meditation of his lately departed wife Alcestis, and quite consuming himself in spiritual contemplation thereof—when suddenly the veiled figure of a woman resembling her in form and gait is led towards him: let us picture his sudden trembling anxiety, his agitated comparisons, his instinctive conviction—and we shall have an analogon to the sensation with which the spectator, excited to Dionysian frenzy, saw the god approaching on the stage, a god with whose sufferings he had already become identified. He involuntarily transferred the entire picture of the god, fluttering magically before his soul, to this masked figure and resolved its reality as it were into a phantasmal unreality. This is the Apollonian dream-state, in which the world of day is veiled, and a new world, clearer, more intelligible, more striking than the former, and nevertheless more shadowy, is ever born anew in perpetual change before our eyes. We accordingly recognise in tragedy a thorough-going stylistic contrast: the language, colour, flexibility and dynamics of the dialogue fall apart in the Dionysian lyrics of the chorus on the one hand, and in the Apollonian dream-world of the scene on the other, into entirely separate spheres of expression. The Apollonian appearances, in which Dionysus objectifies himself, are no longer "ein ewiges Meer, ein wechselnd Weben, ein glühend Leben,"* as is the music of the chorus, they are no longer the forces merely felt, but not condensed into a picture, by which the inspired votary of Dionysus divines the proximity of his god: the clearness and firmness of epic form now speak to him from the scene, Dionysus now no longer speaks through forces, but as an epic hero, almost in the language of Homer.

9.

Whatever rises to the surface in the dialogue of the Apollonian part of Greek tragedy, appears simple, transparent, beautiful. In this sense the dialogue is a copy of the Hellene, whose nature reveals itself in the dance, because in the dance the greatest energy is merely potential, but betrays itself nevertheless in flexible and vivacious movements. The language of the Sophoclean heroes, for instance, surprises us by its Apollonian precision and clearness, so that we at once imagine we see into the innermost recesses of their being, and marvel not a little that the way to these recesses is so short. But if for the moment we disregard the character of the hero which rises to the surface and grows visible—and which at bottom is nothing but the light-picture cast on a dark

* An eternal sea, A weaving, flowing, Life, all glowing. *Faust,* trans. of Bayard Taylor.—TR.

wall, that is, appearance through and through,—if rather we enter into the myth which projects itself in these bright mirrorings, we shall of a sudden experience a phenomenon which bears a reverse relation to one familiar in optics. When, after a vigorous effort to gaze into the sun, we turn away blinded, we have dark-coloured spots before our eyes as restoratives, so to speak; while, on the contrary, those light-picture phenomena of the Sophoclean hero,—in short, the Apollonian of the mask,—are the necessary productions of a glance into the secret and terrible things of nature, as it were shining spots to heal the eye which dire night has seared. Only in this sense can we hope to be able to grasp the true meaning of the serious and significant notion of "Greek cheerfulness"; while of course we encounter the misunderstood notion of this cheerfulness, as resulting from a state of unendangered comfort, on all the ways and paths of the present time.

The most sorrowful figure of the Greek stage, the hapless *Œdipus,* was understood by Sophocles as the noble man, who in spite of his wisdom was destined to error and misery, but nevertheless through his extraordinary sufferings ultimately exerted a magical, wholesome influence on all around him, which continues effective even after his death. The noble man does not sin; this is what the thoughtful poet wishes to tell us: all laws, all natural order, yea, the moral world itself, may be destroyed through his action, but through this very action a higher magic circle of influences is brought into play, which establish a new world on the ruins of the old that has been overthrown. This is what the poet, in so far as he is at the same time a religious thinker, wishes to tell us: as poet, he shows us first of all a wonderfully complicated legal mystery, which the judge slowly unravels, link by link, to his own destruction. The truly Hellenic delight at this dialectical loosening is so great, that a touch of surpassing cheerfulness is thereby communicated to the entire play, which everywhere blunts the edge of the horrible presuppositions of the procedure. In the "Œdipus at Colonus" we find the same cheerfulness, elevated, however, to an infinite transfiguration: in contrast to the aged king, subjected to an excess of misery, and exposed solely as a *sufferer* to all that befalls him, we have here a supermundane cheerfulness, which descends from a divine sphere and intimates to us that in his purely passive attitude the hero attains his highest activity, the influence of which extends far beyond his life, while his earlier conscious musing and striving led him only to passivity. Thus, then, the legal knot of the fable of Œdipus, which to mortal eyes appears indissolubly entangled, is slowly unravelled—and the profoundest human joy comes upon us in the presence of this divine counterpart of dialectics. If this explanation does justice to the poet, it may still be asked whether the substance of the myth is thereby exhausted; and here it turns out that the entire conception of the poet is nothing but the light-picture which healing nature holds up to us after a glance into the abyss. Œdipus, the murderer of his father, the husband of his mother, Œdipus, the interpreter of the riddle of the Sphinx! What does the mysterious triad of these deeds of destiny tell us? There is a primitive popular belief, especially in Persia, that a wise Magian can be born only of incest: which we have forthwith to interpret to ourselves with reference to the riddle-solving and mother-marrying Œdipus, to the effect that when the boundary of the present and future, the rigid law of individuation and, in general, the intrinsic spell of nature, are broken by prophetic and magical powers, an extraordinary counter-naturalness—as, in this case, incest—must have preceded as a cause; for how else could one force nature to surrender her secrets but by victoriously opposing her, *i.e.,* by means of the Unnatural? It is this intuition which I see imprinted in the awful triad of the destiny of Œdipus: the very man who solves the riddle of nature—that double-constituted Sphinx—must also, as the murderer of his father and husband of his mother, break the holiest laws of nature. Indeed, it seems as if the myth sought to whisper into our ears that wisdom, especially Dionysian wisdom, is an unnatural abomination, and that whoever, through his knowledge, plunges nature into an abyss of annihilation, must also experience the dissolution of nature in himself. "The sharpness of wisdom turns round upon the sage: wisdom is a crime against nature": such terrible expressions does the myth call out to us: but the Hellenic poet touches like a sunbeam the sublime and formidable Memnonian statue of the myth, so that it suddenly begins to sound—in Sophoclean melodies.

With the glory of passivity I now contrast the glory of activity which illuminates the *Prometheus* of Æschylus. That which Æschylus the thinker had to tell us here, but which as a poet he only allows us to surmise by his symbolic picture, the youthful Goethe succeeded in disclosing to us in the daring words of his Prometheus:—

"Hier sitz' ich, forme Menschen
Nach meinem Bilde,
Ein Geschlecht, das mir gleich sei,
Zu leiden, zu weinen,
Zu geniessen und zu freuen sich,
Und dein nicht zu achten,
Wie ich!"*

---

* "Here sit I, forming mankind
In my image,
A race resembling me,—
To sorrow and to weep,
To taste, to hold, to enjoy,
And not have need of thee,
As I!"
(Translation in Hæckel's *History of the Evolution of Man.*)

Man, elevating himself to the rank of the Titans, acquires his culture by his own efforts, and compels the gods to unite with him, because in his self-sufficient wisdom he has their existence and their limits in his hand. What is most wonderful, however, in this Promethean form, which according to its fundamental conception is the specific hymn of impiety, is the profound Æschylean yearning for *justice*: the untold sorrow of the bold "single-handed being" on the one hand, and the divine need, ay, the foreboding of a twilight of the gods, on the other, the power of these two worlds of suffering constraining to reconciliation, to metaphysical oneness—all this suggests most forcibly the central and main position of the Æschylean view of things, which sees Moira as eternal justice enthroned above gods and men. In view of the astonishing boldness with which Æschylus places the Olympian world on his scales of justice, it must be remembered that the deep-minded Greek had an immovably firm substratum of metaphysical thought in his mysteries, and that all his sceptical paroxysms could be discharged upon the Olympians. With reference to these deities, the Greek artist, in particular, had an obscure feeling as to mutual dependency: and it is just in the Prometheus of Æschylus that this feeling is symbolised. The Titanic artist found in himself the daring belief that he could create men and at least destroy Olympian deities: namely, by his superior wisdom, for which, to be sure, he had to atone by eternal suffering. The splendid "can-ing" of the great genius, bought too cheaply even at the price of eternal suffering, the stern pride of the *artist*: this is the essence and soul of Æschylean poetry, while Sophocles in his Œdipus preludingly strikes up the victory-song of the *saint*. But even this interpretation which Æschylus has given to the myth does not fathom its astounding depth of terror; the fact is rather that the artist's delight in unfolding, the cheerfulness of artistic creating bidding defiance to all calamity, is but a shining stellar and nebular image reflected in a black sea of sadness. The tale of Prometheus is an original possession of the entire Aryan family of races, and documentary evidence of their capacity for the profoundly tragic; indeed, it is not improbable that this myth has the same characteristic significance for the Aryan race that the myth of the fall of man has for the Semitic, and that there is a relationship between the two myths like that of brother and sister. The presupposition of the Promethean myth is the transcendent value which a naïve humanity attach to *fire* as the true palladium of every ascending culture: that man, however, should dispose at will of this fire, and should not receive it only as a gift from heaven, as the igniting lightning or the warming solar flame, appeared to the contemplative primordial men as crime and robbery of the divine nature. And thus the first philosophical problem at once causes a painful, irreconcilable antagonism between man and God, and puts as it were a mass of rock at the gate of every culture. The best and highest that men can acquire they obtain by a crime, and must now in their turn take upon themselves its consequences, namely the whole flood of sufferings and sorrows with which the offended celestials *must* visit the nobly aspiring race of man: a bitter reflection, which, by the *dignity* it confers on crime, contrasts strangely with the Semitic myth of the fall of man, in which curiosity, beguilement, seducibility, wantonness,—in short, a whole series of pre-eminently feminine passions,—were regarded as the origin of evil. What distinguishes the Aryan representation is the sublime view of *active sin* as the properly Promethean virtue, which suggests at the same time the ethical basis of pessimistic tragedy as the *justification* of human evil—of human guilt as well as of the suffering incurred thereby. The misery in the essence of things—which the contemplative Aryan is not disposed to explain away—the antagonism in the heart of the world, manifests itself to him as a medley of different worlds, for instance, a Divine and a human world, each of which is in the right individually, but as a separate existence alongside of another has to suffer for its individuation. With the heroic effort made by the individual for universality, in his attempt to pass beyond the bounds of individuation and become the *one* universal being, he experiences in himself the primordial contradiction concealed in the essence of things, *i.e.*, he trespasses and suffers. Accordingly crime* is understood by the Aryans to be a man, sin† by the Semites a woman; as also, the original crime is committed by man, the original sin by woman. Besides, the witches' chorus says:

"Wir nehmen das nicht so genau:
Mit tausend Schritten macht's die Frau;
Doch wie sie auch sich eilen kann
Mit einem Sprunge macht's der Mann."‡

He who understands this innermost core of the tale of Prometheus—namely the necessity of crime imposed on the titanically striving individual—will at once be conscious of the un-Apollonian nature of this pessimistic representation: for Apollo seeks to pacify individual beings precisely by drawing boundary lines between them, and by again and again calling attention thereto, with his requirements of self-knowledge and due proportion, as the holiest laws of the universe. In order, however, to prevent the form from congealing to Egyptian rigidity and coldness in consequence of this Apollonian tendency, in order to prevent the extinction of the motion of the entire lake in the effort to prescribe to the individual wave its path and compass, the high tide of the Dionysian tendency destroyed from time to time all the little circles in which the one-sided Apollonian "will" sought to confine the Hellenic world.

---

* *Der* Frevel.

† *Die* Sünde.

‡ We do not measure with such care:
Woman in thousand steps is there,
But howsoe'er she hasten may.
Man in one leap has cleared the way.
Faust, trans. of Bayard Taylor.—TR.

The suddenly swelling tide of the Dionysian then takes the separate little wave-mountains of individuals on its back, just as the brother of Prometheus, the Titan Atlas, does with the earth. This Titanic impulse, to become as it were the Atlas of all individuals, and to carry them on broad shoulders higher and higher, farther and farther, is what the Promethean and the Dionysian have in common. In this respect the Æschylean Prometheus is a Dionysian mask, while, in the afore-mentioned profound yearning for justice, Æschylus betrays to the intelligent observer his paternal descent from Apollo, the god of individuation and of the boundaries of justice. And so the double-being of the Æschylean Prometheus, his conjoint Dionysian and Apollonian nature, might be thus expressed in an abstract formula: "Whatever exists is alike just and unjust, and equally justified in both."

Das ist deine Welt! Das heisst eine Welt!*

10.

It is an indisputable tradition that Greek tragedy in its earliest form had for its theme only the sufferings of Dionysus, and that for some time the only stage-hero therein was simply Dionysus himself. With the same confidence, however, we can maintain that not until Euripides did Dionysus cease to be the tragic hero, and that in fact all the celebrated figures of the Greek stage—Prometheus, Œdipus, etc.—are but masks of this original hero, Dionysus. The presence of a god behind all these masks is the one essential cause of the typical "ideality," so oft exciting wonder, of these celebrated figures. Some one, I know not whom, has maintained that all individuals are comic as individuals and are consequently un-tragic: from whence it might be inferred that the Greeks in general *could* not endure individuals on the tragic stage. And they really seem to have had these sentiments: as, in general, it is to be observed that the Platonic discrimination and valuation of the "idea" in contrast to the "eidolon," the image, is deeply rooted in the Hellenic being. Availing ourselves of Plato's terminology, however, we should have to speak of the tragic figures of the Hellenic stage somewhat as follows. The one truly real Dionysus appears in a multiplicity of forms, in the mask of a fighting hero and entangled, as it were, in the net of an individual will. As the visibly appearing god now talks and acts, he resembles an erring, striving, suffering individual: and that, in general, he *appears* with such epic precision and clearness, is due to the dream-reading Apollo, who reads to the chorus its Dionysian state through this symbolic appearance. In reality, however, this hero is the suffering Dionysus of the mysteries, a god experiencing in himself the sufferings of individuation, of whom wonderful myths tell that as a boy he was dismembered by the Titans

* This is thy world, and what a world!—*Faust.*

and has been worshipped in this state as Zagreus:* whereby is intimated that this dismemberment, the properly Dionysian *suffering,* is like a transformation into air, water, earth, and fire, that we must therefore regard the state of individuation as the source and primal cause of all suffering, as something objectionable in itself. From the smile of this Dionysus sprang the Olympian gods, from his tears sprang man. In his existence as a dismembered god, Dionysus has the dual nature of a cruel barbarised demon, and a mild pacific ruler. But the hope of the epopts looked for a new birth of Dionysus, which we have now to conceive of in anticipation as the end of individuation: it was for this coming third Dionysus that the stormy jubilation-hymns of the epopts resounded. And it is only this hope that sheds a ray of joy upon the features of a world torn asunder and shattered into individuals: as is symbolised in the myth by Demeter sunk in eternal sadness, who *rejoices* again only when told. that she may *once more* give birth to Dionysus In the views of things here given we already have all the elements of a profound and pessimistic contemplation of the world, and along with these we have the *mystery doctrine of tragedy*: the fundamental knowledge of the oneness of all existing things, the consideration of individuation as the primal cause of evil, and art as the joyous hope that the spell of individuation may be broken, as the augury of a restored oneness.

It has already been intimated that the Homeric epos is the poem of Olympian culture, wherewith this culture has sung its own song of triumph over the terrors of the war of the Titans. Under the predominating influence of tragic poetry, these Homeric myths are now reproduced anew, and show by this metempsychosis that meantime the Olympian culture also has been vanquished by a still deeper view of things. The haughty Titan Prometheus has announced to his Olympian tormentor that the extremest danger will one day menace his rule, unless he ally with him betimes. In Æschylus we perceive the terrified Zeus, apprehensive of his end, in alliance with the Titan. Thus, the former age of the Titans is subsequently brought from Tartarus once more to the light of day. The philosophy of wild and naked nature beholds with the undissembled mien of truth the myths of the Homeric world as they dance past: they turn pale, they tremble before the lightning glance of this goddess—till the powerful fist† of the Dionysian artist forces them into the service of the new deity. Dionysian truth takes over the entire domain of myth as symbolism of *its*knowledge, which it makes known partly in the public cult of tragedy and partly in the secret celebration of the dramatic mysteries, always, however, in the old mythical garb. What was the power, which freed Prometheus from his vultures and transformed the myth into a vehicle of Dionysian wisdom? It is the Heracleian power of music: which, having reached its highest

* See article by Mr. Arthur Symons in *The Academy,* 30th August 1902.

† Die mächtige Faust.—Cf. *Faust,* Chorus of Spirits.—TR.

manifestness in tragedy, can invest myths with a new and most profound significance, which we have already had occasion to characterise as the most powerful faculty of music. For it is the fate of every myth to insinuate itself into the narrow limits of some alleged historical reality, and to be treated by some later generation as a solitary fact with historical claims: and the Greeks were already fairly on the way to restamp the whole of their mythical juvenile dream sagaciously and arbitrarily into a historico-pragmatical *juvenile history.* For this is the manner in which religions are wont to die out: when of course under the stern, intelligent eyes of an orthodox dogmatism, the mythical presuppositions of a religion are systematised as a completed sum of historical events, and when one begins apprehensively to defend the credibility of the myth, while at the same time opposing all continuation of their natural vitality and luxuriance; when, accordingly, the feeling for myth dies out, and its place is taken by the claim of religion to historical foundations. This dying myth was now seized by the new-born genius of Dionysian music, in whose hands it bloomed once more, with such colours as it had never yet displayed, with a fragrance that awakened a longing anticipation of a metaphysical world. After this final effulgence it collapses, its leaves wither, and soon the scoffing Lucians of antiquity catch at the discoloured and faded flowers which the winds carry off in every direction. Through tragedy the myth attains its profoundest significance, its most expressive form; it rises once more like a wounded hero, and the whole surplus of vitality, together with the philosophical calmness of the Dying, burns in its eyes with a last powerful gleam.

What meantest thou, oh impious Euripides, in seeking once more to enthral this dying one? It died under thy ruthless hands: and then thou madest use of counterfeit, masked myth, which like the ape of Heracles could only trick itself out in the old finery. And as myth died in thy hands, so also died the genius of music; though thou couldst covetously plunder all the gardens of music—thou didst only realise a counterfeit, masked music. And because thou hast forsaken Dionysus. Apollo hath also forsaken thee; rout up all the passions from their haunts and conjure them into thy sphere, sharpen and polish a sophistical dialectics for the speeches of thy heroes—thy very heroes have only counterfeit, masked passions, and speak only counterfeit, masked music.

11.

Greek tragedy had a fate different from that of all her older sister arts: she died by suicide, in consequence of an irreconcilable conflict; accordingly she died tragically, while they all passed away very calmly and beautifully in ripe old age. For if it be in accordance with a happy state of things to depart this life without a struggle, leaving behind a fair posterity, the closing period of these older arts exhibits such a happy state of things: slowly they sink out of sight, and before their dying eyes already stand their fairer progeny, who impatiently lift up their heads with courageous mien. The death of Greek tragedy, on the other hand, left an immense void, deeply felt everywhere. Even as certain Greek sailors in the time of Tiberius once heard upon a lonesome island the thrilling cry, "great Pan is dead": so now as it were sorrowful wailing sounded through the Hellenic world: "Tragedy is dead! Poetry itself has perished with her! Begone, begone, ye stunted, emaciated epigones! Begone to Hades, that ye may for once eat your fill of the crumbs of your former masters!"

But when after all a new Art blossomed forth which revered tragedy as her ancestress and mistress, it was observed with horror that she did indeed bear the features of her mother, but those very features the latter had exhibited in her long death-struggle. It was *Euripides* who fought this death-struggle of tragedy; the later art is known as the *New Attic Comedy.* In it the degenerate form of tragedy lived on as a monument of the most painful and violent death of tragedy proper.

This connection between the two serves to explain the passionate attachment to Euripides evinced by the poets of the New Comedy, and hence we are no longer surprised at the wish of Philemon, who would have got himself hanged at once, with the sole design of being able to visit Euripides in the lower regions: if only he could be assured generally that the deceased still had his wits. But if we desire, as briefly as possible, and without professing to say aught exhaustive on the subject, to characterise what Euripides has in common with Menander and Philemon, and what appealed to them so strongly as worthy of imitation: it will suffice to say that the *spectator* was brought upon the stage by Euripides. He who has perceived the material of which the Promethean tragic writers prior to Euripides formed their heroes, and how remote from their purpose it was to bring the true mask of reality on the stage, will also know what to make of the wholly divergent tendency of Euripides. Through him the commonplace individual forced his way from the spectators' benches to the stage itself; the mirror in which formerly only great and bold traits found expression now showed the painful exactness that conscientiously reproduces even the abortive lines of nature. Odysseus, the typical Hellene of the Old Art, sank, in the hands of the new poets, to the figure of the Græculus, who, as the good-naturedly cunning domestic slave, stands henceforth in the centre of dramatic interest. What Euripides takes credit for in the Aristophanean "Frogs," namely, that by his household remedies he freed tragic art from its pompous corpulency, is apparent above all in his tragic heroes. The spectator now virtually saw and heard his double on the Euripidean stage, and rejoiced that he could talk so well. But this joy was not all: one even learned of Euripides how to speak: he prides himself upon this in his contest with Æschylus: how the people have learned from him how to observe, debate, and draw conclusions according to the rules of art and with the cleverest sophistications. In general it may be said that through this revolution of the popular language he made the New Comedy possible. For it was henceforth no longer a secret, how—and with what saws—the commonplace could represent and express itself on the stage. Civic mediocrity, on which Euripides built all his political hopes, was now suffered to speak, while heretofore the demigod in tragedy and the drunken satyr, or demiman, in comedy, had determined the character of the language. And so the Aristophanean Euripides prides himself on having portrayed the common, familiar, everyday life and dealings of the people, concerning which all are qualified to pass judgment. If now the entire populace philosophises, manages land and goods with unheard-of circumspection, and conducts law-suits, he takes all the credit to himself, and glories in the splendid results of the wisdom with which he inoculated the rabble.

It was to a populace prepared and enlightened in this manner that the New Comedy could now address itself, of which Euripides had become as it were the chorus-master; only that in this case the chorus of spectators had to be trained. As soon as this chorus was trained to sing in the Euripidean key, there arose that chesslike variety of the drama, the New Comedy, with its perpetual triumphs of cunning and artfulness. But Euripides—the chorus-master—was praised incessantly: indeed, people would have killed themselves in order to learn yet more from him, had they not known that tragic poets were quite as dead as tragedy. But with it the Hellene had surrendered the belief in his immortality; not only the belief in an ideal past, but also the belief in an ideal future. The saying taken from the well-known epitaph, "as an old man, frivolous and capricious," applies also to aged Hellenism. The passing moment, wit, levity, and caprice, are its highest deities; the fifth class, that of the slaves, now attains to power, at least in sentiment: and if we can still speak at all of "Greek cheerfulness," it is the cheerfulness of the slave who has nothing of consequence to answer for, nothing great to strive for, and cannot value anything of the past or future higher than the present. It was this semblance of "Greek cheerfulness" which so revolted the deep-minded and formidable natures of the first four centuries of Christianity: this womanish flight from earnestness and terror, this cowardly contentedness with easy pleasure, was not only contemptible to them, but seemed to be a specifically anti-Christian sentiment. And we must ascribe it to its influence that the conception of Greek antiquity, which lived on for centuries, preserved with almost enduring persistency that peculiar hectic colour of cheerfulness—as if there had never been a Sixth Century with its birth of tragedy, its Mysteries, its Pythagoras and Heraclitus, indeed as if the art-works of that great period did not at all exist, which in fact—each by itself—can in no wise be explained as having sprung from the soil of such a decrepit and slavish love of existence and cheerfulness, and point to an altogether different conception of things as their source.

The assertion made a moment ago, that Euripides introduced the spectator on the stage to qualify him the better to pass judgment on the drama, will make it appear as if the old tragic art was always in a false relation to the spectator: and one would be tempted to extol the radical tendency of Euripides to bring about an adequate relation between art-work and public as an advance on Sophocles. But, as things are, "public" is merely a word, and not at all a homogeneous and constant quantity. Why should the artist be under obligations to accommodate himself to a power whose strength is merely in numbers? And if by virtue of his endowments and aspirations he feels himself superior to every one of these spectators, how could he feel greater respect for the collective expression of all these subordinate capacities than for the relatively highest-endowed individual spectator? In truth, if ever a Greek artist treated his public throughout a long life with presumptuousness and self-sufficiency, it was Euripides, who, even when the masses threw themselves at his feet, with sublime defiance made an open assault on his own tendency, the very tendency with which he had triumphed over the masses. If this genius had had the slightest reverence for the pandemonium of the public, he would have broken down long before the middle of his career beneath the weighty blows of his own failures. These considerations here make it obvious that our formula—namely, that Euripides brought the spectator upon the stage, in order to make him truly competent to pass judgment—was but a provisional one, and that we must seek for a deeper understanding of his tendency. Conversely, it is undoubtedly well known that Æschylus and Sophocles, during all their lives, indeed, far beyond their lives, enjoyed the full favour of the people, and that therefore in the case of these predecessors of Euripides the idea of a false relation between art-work and public was altogether excluded. What was it that thus forcibly diverted this highly gifted artist, so incessantly impelled to production, from the path over which shone the sun of the greatest names in poetry and the cloudless heaven of popular favour? What strange consideration for the spectator led him to defy, the spectator? How could he, owing to too much respect for the public —dis-respect the public?

Euripides—and this is the solution of the riddle just propounded—felt himself, as a poet, undoubtedly superior to the masses, but not to two of his spectators: he brought the masses upon the stage; these two spectators he revered as the only competent judges and masters of his art: in compliance with their directions and admonitions, he transferred the entire world of sentiments, passions, and experiences, hitherto present at every festival representation as the invisible chorus on the spectators' benches, into the souls of his stage-heroes; he yielded to their demands when he also sought for these new characters the new word and the new tone; in their voices alone he heard the conclusive verdict on his work, as also the cheering promise of triumph when he found himself condemned as usual by the justice of the public.

Of these two, spectators the one is—Euripides himself, Euripides *as thinker,* not as poet. It might be said of him, that his unusually large fund of critical ability, as in the case of Lessing, if it did not create, at least constantly fructified a productively artistic collateral impulse. With this faculty, with all the clearness and dexterity of his critical thought, Euripides had sat in the theatre and striven to recognise in the masterpieces of his great predecessors, as in faded paintings, feature and feature, line and line. And here had happened to him what one initiated in the deeper arcana of Æschylean tragedy must needs have expected: he observed something incommensurable in every feature and in every line, a certain deceptive distinctness and at the same time an enigmatic profundity, yea an infinitude, of background. Even the clearest figure had always a comet's tail attached to it, which seemed to suggest the uncertain and the inexplicable. The same twilight shrouded the structure of the drama, especially the significance of the chorus. And how doubtful seemed the solution of the ethical problems to his mind! How questionable the treatment of the myths! How unequal the distribution of happiness and misfortune! Even in the language of the Old Tragedy there was much that was objectionable to him, or at least enigmatical; he found especially too much pomp for simple affairs, too many tropes and immense things for the plainness of the characters. Thus he sat restlessly pondering in the theatre, and as a spectator he acknowledged to himself that he did not understand his great predecessors. If, however, he thought the understanding the root proper of all enjoyment and productivity, he had to inquire and look about to see whether any one else thought as he did, and also acknowledged this incommensurability. But most people, and among them the best individuals, had only a distrustful smile for him, while none could explain why the great masters were still in the right in face of his scruples and objections. And in this painful condition he found *that other spectator,* who did not comprehend, and therefore did not esteem, tragedy. In alliance with him he could venture, from amid his lonesomeness, to begin the prodigious struggle against the art of Æschylus and Sophocles—not with polemic writings, but as a dramatic poet, who opposed *his own* conception of tragedy to the traditional one.

12.

Before we name this other spectator, let us pause here a moment in order to recall our own impression, as previously described, of the discordant and incommensurable elements in the nature of Æschylean tragedy. Let us think of our own astonishment at the *chorus* and the *tragic hero* of that type of tragedy, neither of which we could reconcile with our practices any more than with tradition—till we rediscovered this duplexity itself as the origin and essence of Greek tragedy, as the expression of two interwoven artistic impulses, *the Apollonian and the Dionysian.*

To separate this primitive and all-powerful Dionysian element from tragedy, and to build up a new and purified form of tragedy on the basis of a non-Dionysian art, morality, and conception of things—such is the tendency of Euripides which now reveals itself to us in a clear light.

In a myth composed in the eve of his life, Euripides himself most urgently propounded to his contemporaries the question as to the value and signification of this tendency. Is the Dionysian entitled to exist at all? Should it not be forcibly rooted out of the Hellenic soil? Certainly, the poet tells us, if only it were possible: but the god Dionysus is too powerful; his most intelligent adversary—like Pentheus in the "Bacchæ"—is unwittingly enchanted by him, and in this enchantment meets his fate. The judgment of the two old sages, Cadmus and Tiresias, seems to be also the judgment of the aged poet: that the reflection of the wisest individuals does not overthrow old popular traditions, nor the perpetually propagating worship of Dionysus, that in fact it behoves us to display at least a diplomatically cautious concern in the presence of such strange forces: where however it is always possible that the god may take offence at such lukewarm participation, and finally change the diplomat—in this case Cadmus—into a dragon. This is what a poet tells us, who opposed Dionysus with heroic valour throughout a long life—in order finally to wind up his career with a glorification of his adversary, and with suicide, like one staggering from giddiness, who, in order to escape the horrible vertigo he can no longer endure, casts himself from a tower. This tragedy—the Bacchæ—is a protest against the practicability of his own tendency; alas, and it has already been put into practice! The surprising thing had happened: when the poet recanted, his tendency had already conquered. Dionysus had already been scared from the tragic stage, and in fact by a demonic power which spoke through Euripides. Even Euripides was, in a certain sense, only a mask: the deity that spoke through him was neither Dionysus nor Apollo, but an altogether new-born demon, called *Socrates.* This is the new antithesis: the Dionysian and the Socratic, and the art-work of Greek tragedy was wrecked on it. What if even Euripides now seeks to comfort us by his recantation? It is of no avail: the most magnificent temple lies in ruins. What avails the lamentation of the destroyer, and his confession that it was the most beautiful of all temples? And even that Euripides has been changed into a dragon as a punishment by the art-critics of all ages—who could be content with this wretched compensation?

Let us now approach this *Socratic* tendency with which Euripides combated and vanquished Æschylean tragedy.

We must now ask ourselves, what could be the ulterior aim of the Euripidean design, which, in the highest ideality of its execution, would found drama exclusively on the non-Dionysian? What other form of drama could there be, if it was not to be born of the womb of music, in the mysterious twilight of the Dionysian? Only *the dramatised epos:* in which Apollonian domain of art the *tragic* effect is of course unattainable. It does not depend on the subject-matter of the events here represented; indeed, I venture to assert that it would have been impossible for Goethe in his projected "Nausikaa" to have rendered tragically effective the suicide of the idyllic being with which he intended to complete the fifth act; so extraordinary is the power of the epic-Apollonian representation, that it charms, before our eyes, the most terrible things by the joy in appearance and in redemption through appearance. The poet of the dramatised epos cannot completely blend with his pictures any more than the epic rhapsodist. He is still just the calm, unmoved embodiment of Contemplation whose wide eyes see the picture *before* them. The actor in this dramatised epos still remains intrinsically rhapsodist: the consecration of inner dreaming is on all his actions, so that he is never wholly an actor.

How, then, is the Euripidean play related to this ideal of the Apollonian drama? Just as the younger rhapsodist is related to the solemn rhapsodist of the old time. The former describes his own character in the Platonic "Ion" as follows: "When I am saying anything sad, my eyes fill with tears; when, however, what I am saying is awful and terrible, then my hair stands on end through fear, and my heart leaps." Here we no longer observe anything of the epic absorption in appearance, or of the unemotional coolness of the true actor, who precisely in his highest activity is wholly appearance and joy in appearance. Euripides is the actor with leaping heart, with hair standing on end; as Socratic thinker he designs the plan, as passionate actor he executes it. Neither in the designing nor in the execution is he an artist pure and simple. And so the Euripidean drama is a thing both cool and fiery, equally capable of freezing and burning; it is impossible for it to attain the Apollonian, effect of the epos, while, on the other hand, it has severed itself as much as possible from Dionysian elements, and now, in order to act at all, it requires new stimulants, which can no longer lie within the sphere of the two unique art-impulses, the Apollonian and the Dionysian. The stimulants are cool, paradoxical *thoughts*, in place of Apollonian intuitions—and fiery *passions*—in place Dionysean ecstasies; and in fact, thoughts and passions very realistically copied, and not at all steeped in the ether of art.

Accordingly, if we have perceived this much, that Euripides did not succeed in establishing the drama exclusively on the Apollonian, but that rather his non-Dionysian inclinations deviated into a naturalistic and inartistic tendency, we shall now be able to approach nearer to the character *æsthetic Socratism.* supreme law of which reads about as follows: "to be beautiful everything must be intelligible," as the parallel to the Socratic proposition, "only the knowing is one virtuous." With this canon in his hands Euripides measured all the separate elements of the drama, and rectified them according to his principle: the language, the characters, the dramaturgic structure, and the choric music. The poetic deficiency and retrogression, which we are so often wont to impute to Euripides in comparison with Sophoclean tragedy, is for the most part the product of this penetrating critical process, this daring intelligibility. The Euripidian *prologue* may serve us as an example of the productivity of this, rationalistic method. Nothing could be more opposed to the technique of our stage than the prologue in the drama of Euripides. For a single person to appear at the outset of the play telling us who he is, what precedes the action, what has happened thus far, yea, what will happen in the course of the play, would be designated by a modern playwright as a wanton and unpardonable abandonment of the effect of suspense. Everything that is about to happen is known beforehand; who then cares to wait for it actually to happen?—considering, moreover, that here there is not by any means the exciting relation of a predicting dream to a reality taking place later on. Euripides speculated quite differently. The effect of tragedy never depended on epic suspense, on the fascinating uncertainty as to what is to happen now and afterwards: but rather on the great rhetoro-lyric scenes in which the passion and dialectics of the chief hero swelled to a broad and mighty stream. Everything was arranged for pathos, not for action: and whatever was not arranged for pathos was regarded as objectionable. But what interferes most with the hearer's pleasurable satisfaction in such scenes is a missing link, a gap in the texture of the previous history. So long as the spectator has to divine the meaning of this or that person, or the presuppositions of this or that conflict of inclinations and intentions, his complete absorption in the doings and sufferings of the chief persons is impossible, as is likewise breathless fellow-feeling and fellow-fearing. The Æschyleo-Sophoclean tragedy employed the most ingenious devices in the first scenes to place in the hands of the spectator as if by chance all the threads requisite for understanding the whole: a trait in which that noble artistry is approved, which as it were masks the *inevitably* formal, and causes it to appear as something accidental. But nevertheless Euripides thought he observed that during these first scenes the spectator was in a strange state of anxiety to make out the problem of the previous history, so that the poetic beauties and pathos of the exposition were lost to him. Accordingly he placed the prologue even before the exposition, and put it in the mouth of a person who could be trusted: some deity had often as it were to guarantee the particulars of the tragedy to the public and remove every doubt as to the reality of the myth: as in the case of Descartes, who could only prove the reality of the empiric world by an appeal to the truthfulness of God and His inability to utter falsehood. Euripides makes use of the same divine truthfulness once more at the close of his drama, in order to ensure to the public the future of his heroes; this is the task of the notorious *deus ex machina.* Between the preliminary and the additional epic spectacle there is the dramatico-lyric present, the "drama" proper.

Thus Euripides as a poet echoes above all his own conscious knowledge; and it is precisely on this account that he occupies such a notable position in the history of Greek art. With reference to his critico-productive activity, he must often have felt that he ought to actualise in the drama the words at the beginning of the essay of Anaxagoras: "In the beginning all things were mixed together; then came the understanding and created order." And if Anaxagoras with his "**νοῦς**" seemed like the first sober person among nothing but drunken philosophers, Euripides may also have conceived his relation to the other tragic poets under a similar figure. As long as the sole ruler and disposer of the universe, the **νοῦς** was still excluded from artistic activity, things were all mixed together in a chaotic, primitive mess;—it is thus Euripides was obliged to think, it is thus he was obliged to condemn the "drunken" poets as the first "sober" one among them. What Sophocles said of Æschylus, that he did what was right, though unconsciously, was surely not in the mind of Euripides: who would have admitted only thus much, that Æschylus, *because* he wrought unconsciously, did what was wrong. So also the divine Plato speaks for the most part only ironically of the creative faculty of the poet, in so far as it is not conscious insight, and places it on a par with the gift of the soothsayer and dream-interpreter; insinuating that the poet is incapable of composing until he has become unconscious and reason has deserted him. Like Plato, Euripides undertook to show to the world the reverse of the "unintelligent" poet; his æsthetic principle that "to be beautiful everything must be known" is, as I have said, the parallel to the Socratic "to be good everything must be known." Accordingly we may regard Euripides as the poet of æsthetic Socratism. Socrates, however, was that *second spectator* who did not comprehend and therefore did not esteem the Old Tragedy; in alliance with him Euripides ventured to be the herald of a new artistic activity. If, then, the Old Tragedy was here destroyed, it follows that æsthetic Socratism was the murderous principle; but in so far as the struggle is directed against the Dionysian element in the old art, we recognise in Socrates the opponent of Dionysus, the new Orpheus who rebels against Dionysus; and although destined to be torn to pieces by the Mænads of the Athenian court, yet puts to flight the overpowerful god himself, who, when he fled from Lycurgus, the king of Edoni, sought refuge in the depths of the ocean—namely, in the mystical flood of a secret cult which gradually overspread the earth.

13.

That Socrates stood in close relationship to Euripides in the tendency of his teaching, did not escape the notice of contemporaneous antiquity; the most eloquent expression of this felicitous insight being the tale current in Athens, that Socrates was accustomed to help Euripides in poetising. Both names were mentioned in one breath by the adherents of the "good old time," whenever they came to enumerating the popular agitators of the day: to whose influence they attributed the fact that the old Marathonian stalwart capacity of body and soul was more and more being sacrificed to a dubious enlightenment, involving progressive degeneration of the physical and mental powers. It is in this tone, half indignantly and half contemptuously, that Aristophanic comedy is wont to speak of both of them—to the consternation of modern men, who would indeed be willing enough to give up Euripides, but cannot suppress their amazement that Socrates should appear in Aristophanes as the first and head *sophist,* as the mirror and epitome of all sophistical tendencies; in connection with which it offers the single consolation of putting Aristophanes himself in the pillory, as a rakish, lying Alcibiades of poetry. Without here defending the profound instincts of Aristophanes against such attacks, I shall now indicate, by means of the sentiments of the time, the close connection between Socrates and Euripides. With this purpose in view, it is especially to be remembered that Socrates, as an opponent of tragic art, did not ordinarily patronise tragedy, but only appeared among the spectators when a new play of Euripides was performed. The most noted thing, however, is the close juxtaposition of the two names in the Delphic oracle, which designated Socrates as the wisest of men, but at the same time decided that the second prize in the contest of wisdom was due to Euripides.

Sophocles was designated as the third in this scale of rank; he who could pride himself that, in comparison with Æschylus, he did what was right, and did it, moreover, because he *knew* what was right. It is evidently just the degree of clearness of this *knowledge,* which distinguishes these three men in common as the three "knowing ones" of their age.

The most decisive word, however, for this new and unprecedented esteem of knowledge and insight was spoken by Socrates when he found that he was the only one who acknowledged to himself that he *knew nothing* while in his critical pilgrimage through Athens, and calling on the greatest statesmen, orators, poets, and artists, he discovered everywhere the conceit of knowledge. He perceived, to his astonishment, that all these celebrities were without a proper and accurate insight, even with regard to their own callings, and practised them only by instinct. "Only by instinct": with this phrase we touch upon the heart and core of the Socratic tendency. Socratism condemns therewith existing art as well as existing ethics; wherever Socratism turns its searching eyes it beholds the lack of insight and the power of illusion; and from this lack infers the inner perversity and objectionableness of existing conditions. From this point onwards, Socrates believed that he was called upon to, correct existence; and, with an air of disregard and superiority, as the precursor of an altogether different culture, art, and morality, he enters single-handed into a world, of which, if we reverently touched the hem, we should count it our greatest happiness.

Here is the extraordinary hesitancy which always seizes upon us with regard to Socrates, and again and again invites us to ascertain the sense and purpose of this most questionable phenomenon of antiquity. Who is it that ventures single-handed to disown the Greek character, which, as Homer, Pindar, and Æschylus, as Phidias, as Pericles, as Pythia and Dionysus, as the deepest abyss and the highest height, is sure of our wondering admiration? What demoniac power is it which would presume to spill this magic draught in the dust? What demigod is it to whom the chorus of spirits of the noblest of mankind must call out: "Weh! Weh! Du hast sie zerstört, die schöne Welt, mit mächtiger Faust; sie stürzt, sie zerfällt!"*

A key to the character of Socrates is presented to us by the surprising phenomenon designated as the "daimonion" of Socrates. In special circumstances, when his gigantic intellect began to stagger, he got a secure support in the utterances of a divine voice which then spake to him. This voice, whenever it comes, always *dissuades.* In this totally abnormal nature instinctive wisdom only appears in order to hinder the progress of conscious perception here and there. While in all productive men it is instinct which is the creatively affirmative force, consciousness only comporting itself critically and dissuasively; with Socrates it is instinct which becomes critic; it is consciousness which becomes creator—a perfect monstrosity *per defectum!* And we do indeed observe here a monstrous *defectus* of all mystical aptitude, so that Socrates might be designated as the specific *non-mystic,* in whom the logical nature is developed, through a superfoetation, to the same excess as instinctive wisdom is developed in the mystic. On the other hand, however, the logical instinct which appeared in Socrates was absolutely prohibited from turning against itself; in its unchecked flow it manifests a native power such as we meet with, to our shocking surprise, only among the very greatest instinctive forces. He who has experienced even a breath of the divine naïveté and security of the Socratic course of life in the Platonic writings, will also feel that the enormous driving-wheel of logical Socratism is in motion, as it were, *behind* Socrates, and that it must be viewed through Socrates as through a shadow. And that he himself had a boding of this relation is apparent from the dignified earnestness with which he everywhere, and even before his judges, insisted on his divine calling. To refute him here was really as impossible as to approve of his instinct-disintegrating influence. In view of this indissoluble conflict, when he had at last been brought before the forum of the Greek state, there was only one punishment demanded, namely exile; he might have been sped across the borders as something thoroughly enigmatical, irrubricable and inexplicable, and so posterity would have been quite unjustified in charging the Athenians with a deed of ignominy. But that the sentence of death, and not mere exile, was pronounced upon him, seems to have been brought about by Socrates himself, with perfect knowledge of the circumstances, and without the natural fear of death: he met his death with the calmness with which,

---

* Woe! Woe!
Thou hast it destroyed,
The beautiful world;
With powerful fist;
In ruin 'tis hurled!
Faust, trans. of Bayard Taylor.—TR.

according to the description of Plato, he leaves the symposium at break of day, as the last of the revellers, to begin a new day; while the sleepy companions remain behind on the benches and the floor, to dream of Socrates, the true eroticist. *The dying Socrates* became the new ideal of the noble Greek youths,—an ideal they had never yet beheld,—and above all, the typical Hellenic youth, Plato, prostrated himself before this scene with all the fervent devotion of his visionary soul.

14.

Let us now imagine the one great Cyclopean eye of Socrates fixed on tragedy, that eye in which the fine frenzy of artistic enthusiasm had never glowed—let us think how it was denied to this eye to gaze with pleasure into the Dionysian abysses—what could it not but see in the "sublime and greatly lauded" tragic art, as Plato called it? Something very absurd, with causes that seemed to be without effects, and effects apparently without causes; the whole, moreover, so motley and diversified that it could not but be repugnant to a thoughtful mind, a dangerous incentive, however, to sensitive and irritable souls. We know what was the sole kind of poetry which he comprehended: the *Æsopian fable*: and he did this no doubt with that smiling complaisance with which the good honest Gellert sings the praise of poetry in the fable of the bee and the hen:—

"Du siehst an mir, wozu sie nützt,

Dem, der nicht viel Verstand besitzt,

Die Wahrheit durch ein Bild zu sagen."*

But then it seemed to Socrates that tragic art did not even "tell the truth": not to mention the fact that it addresses itself to him who "hath but little wit"; consequently not to the philosopher: a twofold reason why it should be avoided. Like Plato, he reckoned it among the seductive arts which only represent the agreeable, not the useful, and hence he required of his disciples abstinence and strict separation from such unphilosophical allurements; with such success that the youthful tragic poet Plato first of all burned his poems to be able to become a scholar of Socrates. But where unconquerable native capacities bore up against the Socratic maxims, their power, together with the momentum of his mighty character, still sufficed to force poetry itself into new and hitherto unknown channels.

An instance of this is the aforesaid Plato: he, who in the condemnation of tragedy and of art in general certainly did not fall short of the naïve cynicism

---

* In me thou seest its benefit,—

To him who hath but little wit,

Through parables to tell the truth.

of his master, was nevertheless constrained by sheer artistic necessity to create a form of art which is inwardly related even to the then existing forms of art which he repudiated. Plato's main objection to the old art—that it is the imitation of a phantom, and hence belongs to a sphere still lower than the empiric world—could not at all apply to the new art: and so we find Plato endeavouring to go beyond reality and attempting to represent the idea which underlies this pseudo-reality. But Plato, the thinker, thereby arrived by a roundabout road just at the point where he had always been at home as poet, and from which Sophocles and all the old artists had solemnly protested against that objection. If tragedy absorbed into itself all the earlier varieties of art, the same could again be said in an unusual sense of Platonic dialogue, which, engendered by a mixture of all the then existing forms and styles, hovers midway between narrative, lyric and drama, between prose and poetry, and has also thereby broken loose from the older strict law of unity of linguistic form; a movement which was carried still farther by the *cynic* writers, who in the most promiscuous style, oscillating to and fro betwixt prose and metrical forms, realised also the literary picture of the "raving Socrates" whom they were wont to represent in life. Platonic dialogue was as it were the boat in which the shipwrecked ancient poetry saved herself together with all her children: crowded into a narrow space and timidly obsequious to the one steersman, Socrates, they now launched into a new world, which never tired of looking at the fantastic spectacle of this procession. In very truth, Plato has given to all posterity the prototype of a new form of art, the prototype of the *novel* which must be designated as the infinitely evolved Æsopian fable, in which poetry holds the same rank with reference to dialectic philosophy as this same philosophy held for many centuries with reference to theology: namely, the rank of*ancilla*. This was the new position of poetry into which Plato forced it under the pressure of the demon-inspired Socrates.

Here *philosophic thought* overgrows art and compels it to cling close to the trunk of dialectics. The *Apollonian* tendency has chrysalised in the logical schematism; just as something analogous in the case of Euripides (and moreover a translation of the *Dionysian* into the naturalistic emotion) was forced upon our attention. Socrates, the dialectical hero in Platonic drama, reminds us of the kindred nature of the Euripidean hero, who has to defend his actions by arguments and counter-arguments, and thereby so often runs the risk of forfeiting our tragic pity; for who could mistake the *optimistic* element in the essence of dialectics, which celebrates a jubilee in every conclusion, and can breathe only in cool clearness and consciousness: the optimistic element, which, having once forced its way into tragedy, must gradually overgrow its Dionysian regions, and necessarily impel it to self-destruction—even to the death-leap into the bourgeois drama. Let us but realise the consequences of the Socratic maxims: "Virtue is knowledge; man only sins from ignorance; he who is virtuous is happy": these three fundamental forms of optimism involve the death of tragedy. For the virtuous hero must now be a dialectician; there must now be a necessary, visible connection between virtue and knowledge, between belief and morality; the transcendental justice of the plot in Æschylus is now degraded to the superficial and audacious principle of poetic justice with its usual *deus ex machina*.

How does the *chorus,* and, in general, the entire Dionyso-musical substratum of tragedy, now appear in the light of this new Socrato-optimistic stage-world? As something accidental, as a readily dispensable reminiscence of the origin of tragedy; while we have in fact seen that the chorus can be understood only as the cause of tragedy, and of the tragic generally. This perplexity with respect to the chorus first manifests itself in Sophocles—an important sign that the Dionysian basis of tragedy already begins to disintegrate with him. He no longer ventures to entrust to the chorus the main share of the effect, but limits its sphere to such an extent that it now appears almost co-ordinate with the actors, just as if it were elevated from the orchestra into the scene: whereby of course its character is completely destroyed, notwithstanding that Aristotle countenances this very theory of the chorus. This alteration of the position of the chorus, which Sophocles at any rate recommended by his practice, and, according to tradition, even by a treatise, is the first step towards the *annihilation* of the chorus, the phases of which follow one another with alarming rapidity in Euripides, Agathon, and the New Comedy. Optimistic dialectics drives, *music* out of tragedy with the scourge of its syllogisms: that is, it destroys the essence of tragedy, which can be explained only as a manifestation and illustration of Dionysian states, as the visible symbolisation of music, as the dream-world of Dionysian ecstasy.

If, therefore, we are to assume an anti-Dionysian tendency operating even before Socrates, which received in him only an unprecedentedly grand expression, we must not shrink from the question as to what a phenomenon like that of Socrates indicates: whom in view of the Platonic dialogues we are certainly not entitled to regard as a purely disintegrating, negative power. And though there can be no doubt whatever that the most immediate effect of the Socratic impulse tended to the dissolution of Dionysian tragedy, yet a profound experience of Socrates' own life compels us to ask whether there is *necessarily* only an antipodal relation between Socratism and art, and whether the birth of an "artistic Socrates" is in general something contradictory in itself.

For that despotic logician had now and then the feeling of a gap, or void, a sentiment of semi-reproach, as of a possibly neglected duty with respect to art. There often came to him, as he tells his friends in prison, one and the same dream-apparition, which kept constantly repeating to him: "Socrates, practise music." Up to his very last days he solaces himself with the opinion that his philosophising is the highest form of poetry, and finds it hard to believe that a deity will remind him of the "common, popular music." Finally, when in prison, he consents to practise also this despised music, in order thoroughly to unburden his conscience. And in this frame of mind he composes a poem on Apollo and turns a few Æsopian fables into verse. It was something similar to the demonian warning voice which urged him to these practices; it was because of his Apollonian insight that, like a barbaric king, he did not understand the noble image of a god and was in danger of sinning against a deity—through ignorance. The prompting voice of the Socratic dream-vision is the only sign of doubtfulness as to the limits of logical nature. "Perhaps "—thus he had to ask himself—"what is not intelligible to me is not therefore unreasonable? Perhaps there is a realm of wisdom from which the logician is banished? Perhaps art is even a necessary correlative of and supplement to science?"

15.

In the sense of these last portentous questions it must now be indicated how the influence of Socrates (extending to the present moment, indeed, to all futurity) has spread over posterity like an ever-increasing shadow in the evening sun, and how this influence again and again necessitates a regeneration of *art,*—yea, of art already with metaphysical, broadest and profoundest sense,—and its own eternity guarantees also the eternity of art.

Before this could be perceived, before the intrinsic dependence of every art on the Greeks, the Greeks from Homer to Socrates, was conclusively demonstrated, it had to happen to us with regard to these Greeks as it happened to the Athenians with regard to Socrates. Nearly every age and stage of culture has at some time or other sought with deep displeasure to free itself from the Greeks, because in their presence everything self-achieved, sincerely admired and apparently quite original, seemed all of a sudden to lose life and colour and shrink to an abortive copy, even to caricature. And so hearty indignation breaks forth time after time against this presumptuous little nation, which dared to designate as "barbaric" for all time everything not native: who are they, one asks one's self, who, though they possessed only an ephemeral historical splendour, ridiculously restricted institutions, a dubious excellence in their customs, and were even branded with ugly vices, yet lay claim to the dignity and singular position among the peoples to which genius is entitled among the masses. What a pity one has not been so fortunate as to find the cup of hemlock with which such an affair could be disposed of without ado: for all the poison which envy, calumny, and rankling resentment engendered within themselves have not sufficed to destroy that self-sufficient grandeur! And so one feels ashamed and afraid in the presence of the Greeks: unless one prize truth above all things, and dare also to acknowledge to one's self this truth, that the Greeks, as charioteers, hold in their hands the reins of our own and of every culture, but that almost always chariot and horses are of too poor material and incommensurate with the glory of their guides, who then will deem it sport to run such a team into an abyss: which they themselves clear with the leap of Achilles.

In order to assign also to Socrates the dignity of such a leading position, it will suffice to recognise in him the type of an unheard-of form of existence, the type of the *theoretical man,* with regard to whose meaning and purpose it will be our next task to attain an insight. Like the artist, the theorist also finds an infinite satisfaction in what *is* and, like the former, he is shielded by this satisfaction from the practical ethics of pessimism with its lynx eyes which shine only in the dark. For if the artist in every unveiling of truth always cleaves with raptured eyes only to that which still remains veiled after the unveiling, the theoretical man, on the other hand, enjoys and contents himself with the cast-off veil, and finds the consummation of his pleasure in the process of a continuously successful unveiling through his own unaided efforts. There would have been no science if it had only been concerned about that *one* naked goddess and nothing else. For then its disciples would have been obliged to feel like those who purposed to dig a hole straight through the earth: each one of whom perceives that with the utmost lifelong exertion he is able to excavate only a very little of the enormous depth, which is again filled up before his eyes by the labours of his successor, so that a third man seems to do well when on his own account he selects a new spot for his attempts at tunnelling. If now some one proves conclusively that the antipodal goal cannot be attained in this direct way, who will still care to toil on in the old depths, unless he has learned to content himself in the meantime with finding precious stones or discovering natural laws? For that reason Lessing, the most honest theoretical man, ventured to say that he cared more for the search after truth than for truth itself: in saying which he revealed the fundamental secret of science, to the astonishment, and indeed, to the vexation of scientific men. Well, to be sure, there stands alongside of this detached perception, as an excess of honesty, if not of presumption, a profound *illusion* which first came to the world in the person of Socrates, the imperturbable belief that, by means of the clue of causality, thinking reaches to the deepest abysses of being, and that thinking is able not only to perceive being but even to *correct* it. This sublime metaphysical illusion is added as an instinct to science and again and again leads the latter to its limits, where it must change into *art; which is really the end, to be attained by this mechanism.*

If we now look at Socrates in the light of this thought, he appears to us as the first who could not only live, but—what is far more—also die under the guidance of this instinct of science: and hence the picture of the *dying, Socrates*, as the man delivered from the fear of death by knowledge and argument, is the escutcheon, above the entrance to science which reminds every one of its mission, namely, to make existence appear to be comprehensible, and therefore to be justified: for which purpose, if arguments do not suffice, *myth* also must be used, which I just now designated even as the necessary consequence, yea, as the end of science.

He who once makes intelligible to himself how, after the death of Socrates, the mystagogue of science, one philosophical school succeeds another, like wave upon wave,—how an entirely unfore-shadowed universal development of the thirst for knowledge in the widest compass of the cultured world (and as the specific task for every one highly gifted) led science on to the high sea from which since then it has never again been able to be completely ousted; how through the universality of this movement a common net of thought was first stretched over the entire globe, with prospects, moreover, of conformity to law in an entire solar system;—he who realises all this, together with the amazingly high pyramid of our present-day knowledge, cannot fail to see in Socrates the turning-point and vortex of so-called universal history. For if one were to imagine the whole incalculable sum of energy which has been used up by that universal tendency,—employed, *not* in the service of knowledge, but for the practical, *i.e.,* egoistical ends of individuals and peoples,—then probably the instinctive love of life would be so much weakened in universal wars of destruction and incessant migrations of peoples, that, owing to the practice of suicide, the individual would perhaps feel the last remnant of a sense of duty, when, like the native of the Fiji Islands, as son he strangles his parents and, as friend, his friend: a practical pessimism which might even give rise to a horrible ethics of general slaughter out of pity—which, for the rest, exists and has existed wherever art in one form or another, especially as science and religion, has not appeared as a remedy and preventive of that pestilential breath.

In view of this practical pessimism, Socrates is the archetype of the theoretical optimist, who in the above-indicated belief in the fathomableness of the nature of things, attributes to knowledge and perception the power of a universal medicine, and sees in error and evil. To penetrate into the depths of the nature of things, and to separate true perception from error and illusion, appeared to the Socratic man the noblest and even the only truly human calling: just as from the time of Socrates onwards the mechanism of concepts, judgments, and inferences was prized above all other capacities as the highest activity and the most admirable gift of nature. Even the sublimest moral acts, the stirrings of pity, of self-sacrifice, of heroism, and that tranquillity of soul, so difficult of attainment, which the Apollonian Greek called Sophrosyne, were derived by Socrates, and his like-minded successors up to the present day, from the dialectics of knowledge, and were accordingly designated as teachable. He who has experienced in himself the joy of a Socratic perception, and felt how it seeks to embrace, in constantly widening circles, the entire world of phenomena, will thenceforth find no stimulus which could urge him to existence more forcible than the desire to complete that conquest and to knit the net impenetrably close. To a person thus minded the Platonic Socrates then appears as the teacher of an entirely new form of "Greek cheerfulness" and felicity of existence, which seeks to discharge itself in actions, and will find its discharge for the most part in maieutic and pedagogic influences on noble youths, with a view to the ultimate production of genius.

But now science, spurred on by its powerful illusion, hastens irresistibly to its limits, on which its optimism, hidden in the essence of logic, is wrecked. For the periphery of the circle of science has an infinite number of points, and while there is still no telling how this circle can ever be completely measured, yet the noble and gifted man, even before the middle of his career, inevitably comes into contact with those extreme points of the periphery where he stares at the inexplicable. When he here sees to his dismay how logic coils round itself at these limits and finally bites its own tail—then the new form of perception discloses itself, namely *tragic perception,* which, in order even to be endured, requires art as a safeguard and remedy.

If, with eyes strengthened and refreshed at the sight of the Greeks, we look upon the highest spheres of the world that surrounds us, we behold the avidity of the insatiate optimistic knowledge, of which Socrates is the typical representative, transformed into tragic resignation and the need of art: while, to be sure, this same avidity, in its lower stages, has to exhibit itself as antagonistic to art, and must especially have an inward detestation of Dionyso-tragic art, as was exemplified in the opposition of Socratism to Æschylean tragedy.

Here then with agitated spirit we knock at the gates of the present and the future: will that "transforming" lead to ever new configurations of genius, and especially of the *music-practising Socrates*? Will the net of art which is spread over existence, whether under the name of religion or of science, be knit always more closely and delicately, or is it destined to be torn to shreds under the restlessly barbaric activity and whirl which is called "the present day"?—Anxious, yet not disconsolate, we stand aloof for a little while, as the spectators who are permitted to be witnesses of these tremendous struggles and transitions. Alas! It is the charm of these struggles that he who beholds them must also fight them!

16.

By this elaborate historical example we have endeavoured to make it clear that tragedy perishes as surely by evanescence of the spirit of music as it can be born only out of this spirit. In order to qualify the singularity of this assertion, and, on the other hand, to disclose the source of this insight of ours, we must now confront with clear vision the analogous phenomena of the present time; we must enter into the midst of these struggles, which, as I said just now, are being carried on in the highest spheres of our present world between the insatiate optimistic perception and the tragic need of art. In so doing I shall leave out of consideration all other antagonistic tendencies which at all times oppose art, especially tragedy, and which at present again extend their sway triumphantly, to such an extent that of the theatrical arts only the farce and the ballet, for example, put forth their blossoms, which perhaps not every one cares to smell, in tolerably rich luxuriance. I will speak only of the *Most Illustrious Opposition* to the tragic conception of things—and by this I mean essentially optimistic science, with its ancestor Socrates at the head of it. Presently also the forces will be designated which seem to me to guarantee *a re-birth of tragedy*—and who knows what other blessed hopes for the German genius!

Before we plunge into the midst of these struggles, let us array ourselves in the armour of our hitherto acquired knowledge. In contrast to all those who are intent on deriving the arts from one exclusive principle, as the necessary vital source of every work of art, I keep my eyes fixed on the two artistic deities of the Greeks, Apollo and Dionysus, and recognise in them the living and conspicuous representatives of *two* worlds of art which differ in their intrinsic essence and in their highest aims. Apollo stands before me as the transfiguring genius of the *principium individuationis* through which alone the redemption in appearance is to be truly attained, while by the mystical cheer of Dionysus the spell of individuation is broken, and the way lies open to the Mothers of Being,* to the innermost heart of things. This extraordinary antithesis, which opens up yawningly between plastic art as the Apollonian and music as the Dionysian art, has become manifest to only one of the great thinkers, to such an extent that, even without this key to the symbolism of the Hellenic divinities, he allowed to music a different character and origin in advance of all the other arts, because, unlike them, it is not a copy of the phenomenon, but a direct copy of the will itself, and therefore represents *the metaphysical of everything physical in the world*, the thing-in-itself of every phenomenon. (Schopenhauer, *Welt als Wille und Vorstellung,* I. 310.) To this most important perception of æsthetics (with which, taken in a serious sense, æsthetics properly commences), Richard Wagner, by way of confirmation of its eternal truth, affixed his seal, when he asserted in his *Beethoven* that music must be judged according to æsthetic principles quite different from those which apply to the plastic arts, and not, in general, according to the category of beauty: although an erroneous æsthetics, inspired by a misled and degenerate art, has by virtue of the concept of beauty prevailing in the plastic domain accustomed itself to demand of music an effect analogous to that of the works of plastic art, namely the suscitating *delight in beautiful forms*. Upon perceiving this extraordinary antithesis, I felt a strong inducement to approach the essence of Greek tragedy, and, by means of it, the profoundest revelation of Hellenic

* Cf. *Faust,* Part II. Act I.—Tr.

genius: for I at last thought myself to be in possession of a charm to enable me—far beyond the phraseology of our usual æsthetics—to represent vividly to my mind the primitive problem of tragedy: whereby such an astounding insight into the Hellenic character was afforded me that it necessarily seemed as if our proudly comporting classico-Hellenic science had thus far contrived to subsist almost exclusively on phantasmagoria and externalities.

Perhaps we may lead up to this primitive problem with the question: what æsthetic effect results when the intrinsically separate art-powers, the Apollonian and the Dionysian, enter into concurrent actions? Or, in briefer form: how is music related to image and concept?—Schopenhauer, whom Richard Wagner, with especial reference to this point, accredits with an unsurpassable clearness and perspicuity of exposition, expresses himself most copiously on the subject in the following passage which I shall cite here at full length* (*Welt als Wille und Vorstellung,* I. p. 309): "According to all this, we may regard the phenomenal world, or nature, and music as two different expressions of the same thing,† which is therefore itself the only medium of the analogy between these two expressions, so that a knowledge of this medium is required in order to understand that analogy. Music, therefore, if regarded as an expression of the world, is in the highest degree a universal language, which is related indeed to the universality of concepts, much as these are related to the particular things. Its universality, however, is by no means the empty universality of abstraction, but of quite a different kind, and is united with thorough and distinct definiteness. In this respect it resembles geometrical figures and numbers, which are the universal forms of all possible objects of experience and applicable to them all *a priori*, and yet are not abstract but perceptiple and thoroughly determinate. All possible efforts, excitements and manifestations of will, all that goes on in the heart of man and that reason includes in the wide, negative concept of feeling, may be expressed by the infinite number of possible melodies, but always in the universality of mere form, without the material, always according to the thing-in-itself, not the phenomenon,—of which they reproduce the very soul and essence as it were, without the body. This deep relation which music bears to the true nature of all things also explains the fact that suitable music played to any scene, action, event, or surrounding seems to disclose to us its most secret meaning, and appears as the most accurate and distinct commentary upon it; as also the fact that whoever gives himself up entirely to the impression of a symphony seems to see all the possible events of life and the world take place in himself: nevertheless upon reflection he can find no likeness between the music and the things that passed before his mind. For, as we have said, music is distinguished from all the other arts by the fact that it is not a copy of the phenomenon, or, more accurately, the

* Cf. *World and Will as Idea,* I. p. 339, trans. by Haldane and Kemp.

† That is "the will" as understood by Schopenhauer.—TR.

adequate objectivity of the will, but the direct copy of the will itself, and therefore represents the metaphysical of everything physical in the world, and the thing-in-itself of every phenomenon. We might, therefore, just as well call the world embodied music as embodied will: and this is the reason why music makes every picture, and indeed every scene of real life and of the world, at once appear with higher significance; all the more so, to be sure, in proportion as its melody is analogous to the inner spirit of the given phenomenon. It rests upon this that we are able to set a poem to music as a song, or a perceptible representation as a pantomime, or both as an opera. Such particular pictures of human life, set to the universal language of music, are never bound to it or correspond to it with stringent necessity, but stand to it only in the relation of an example chosen at will to a general concept. In the determinateness of the real they represent that which music expresses in the universality of mere form. For melodies are to a certain extent, like general concepts, an abstraction from the actual. This actual world, then, the world of particular things, affords the object of perception, the special and the individual, the particular case, both to the universality of concepts and to the universality of the melodies. But these two universalities are in a certain respect opposed to each other, for the concepts contain only the forms, which are first of all abstracted from perception,—the separated outward shell of things, as it were,—and hence they are, in the strictest sense of the term, *abstracta*; music, on the other hand, gives the inmost kernel which precedes all forms, or the heart of things. This relation may be very well expressed in the language of the schoolmen, by saying: the concepts are the *universalia post rem,* but music gives the *universalia ante rem,* and the real world the *universalia in re.*—But that in general a relation is possible between a composition and a perceptible representation rests, as we have said, upon the fact that both are simply different expressions of the same inner being of the world. When now, in the particular case, such a relation is actually given, that is to say, when the composer has been able to express in the universal language of music the emotions of will which constitute the heart of an event, then the melody of the song, the music of the opera, is expressive. But the analogy discovered by the composer between the two must have proceeded from the direct knowledge of the nature of the world unknown to his reason, and must not be an imitation produced with conscious intention by means of conceptions; otherwise the music does not express the inner nature of the will itself, but merely gives an inadequate imitation of its phenomenon: all specially imitative music does this."

We have therefore, according to the doctrine of Schopenhauer, an immediate understanding of music as the language of the will, and feel our imagination stimulated to give form to this invisible and yet so actively stirred spirit-world which speaks to us, and prompted to embody it in an analogous example. On the other hand, image and concept, under the influence of a truly conformable music, acquire a higher significance. Dionysian art therefore is wont to exercise—two kinds of influences, on the Apollonian art-faculty: music firstly incites to the *symbolic intuition* of Dionysian universality, and, secondly, it causes the symbolic image to stand forth *in its fullest significance.* From these facts, intelligible in themselves and not inaccessible to profounder observation, I infer the capacity of music to give birth to *myth,* that is to say, the most significant exemplar, and precisely *tragic* myth: the myth which speaks of Dionysian knowledge in symbols. In the phenomenon of the lyrist, I have set forth that in him music strives to express itself with regard to its nature in Apollonian images. If now we reflect that music in its highest potency must seek to attain also to its highest symbolisation, we must deem it possible that it also knows how to find the symbolic expression of its inherent Dionysian wisdom; and where shall we have to seek for this expression if not in tragedy and, in general, in the conception of the *tragic*?

From the nature of art, as it is ordinarily conceived according to the single category of appearance and beauty, the tragic cannot be honestly deduced at all; it is only through the spirit of music that we understand the joy in the annihilation of the individual. For in the particular examples of such annihilation only is the eternal phenomenon of Dionysian art made clear to us, which gives expression to the will in its omnipotence, as it were, behind the *principium individuationis,* the eternal life beyond all phenomena, and in spite of all annihilation. The metaphysical delight in the tragic is a translation of the instinctively unconscious Dionysian wisdom into the language of the scene: the hero, the highest manifestation of the will, is disavowed for our pleasure, because he is only phenomenon, and because the eternal life of the will is not affected by his annihilation. "We believe in eternal life," tragedy exclaims; while music is the proximate idea of this life. Plastic art has an altogether different object: here Apollo vanquishes the suffering of the individual by the radiant glorification of the *eternity of the phenomenon*; here beauty triumphs over the suffering inherent in life; pain is in a manner surreptitiously obliterated from the features of nature. In Dionysian art and its tragic symbolism the same nature speaks to us with its true undissembled voice: "Be as I am! Amidst the ceaseless change of phenomena the eternally creative primordial mother, eternally impelling to existence, self-satisfying eternally with this change of phenomena!"

17.

Dionysian art, too, seeks to convince us of the eternal joy of existence: only we are to seek this joy not in phenomena, but behind phenomena. We are to perceive how all that comes into being must be ready for a sorrowful end; we are compelled to look into the terrors of individual existence—yet we are not to become torpid: a metaphysical comfort tears us momentarily from the bustle of the transforming figures. We are really for brief moments Primordial

Being itself, and feel its indomitable desire for being and joy in existence; the struggle, the pain, the destruction of phenomena, now appear to us as something necessary, considering the surplus of innumerable forms of existence which throng and push one another into life, considering the exuberant fertility of the universal will. We are pierced by the maddening sting of these pains at the very moment when we have become, as it were, one with the immeasurable primordial joy in existence, and when we anticipate, in Dionysian ecstasy, the indestructibility and eternity of this joy. In spite of fear and pity, we are the happy living beings, not as individuals, but as the *one* living being, with whose procreative joy we are blended.

The history of the rise of Greek tragedy now tells us with luminous precision that the tragic art of the Greeks was really born of the spirit of music: with which conception we believe we have done justice for the first time to the original and most astonishing significance of the chorus. At the same time, however, we must admit that the import of tragic myth as set forth above never became transparent with sufficient lucidity to the Greek poets, let alone the Greek philosophers; their heroes speak, as it were, more superficially than they act; the myth does not at all find its adequate objectification in the spoken word. The structure of the scenes and the conspicuous images reveal a deeper wisdom than the poet himself can put into words and concepts: the same being also observed in Shakespeare, whose Hamlet, for instance, in an analogous manner talks more superficially than he acts, so that the previously mentioned lesson of Hamlet is to be gathered not from his words, but from a more profound contemplation and survey of the whole. With respect to Greek tragedy, which of course presents itself to us only as word-drama, I have even intimated that the incongruence between myth and expression might easily tempt us to regard it as shallower and less significant than it really is, and accordingly to postulate for it a more superficial effect than it must have had according to the testimony of the ancients: for how easily one forgets that what the word-poet did not succeed in doing, namely realising the highest spiritualisation and ideality of myth, he might succeed in doing every moment as creative musician! We require, to be sure, almost by philological method to reconstruct for ourselves the ascendency of musical influence in order to receive something of the incomparable comfort which must be characteristic of true tragedy. Even this musical ascendency, however, would only have been felt by us as such had we been Greeks: while in the entire development of Greek music—as compared with the infinitely richer music known and familiar to us—we imagine we hear only the youthful song of the musical genius intoned with a feeling of diffidence. The Greeks are, as the Egyptian priests say, eternal children, and in tragic art also they are only children who do not know what a sublime plaything has originated under their hands and—is being demolished.

That striving of the spirit of music for symbolic and mythical manifestation, which increases from the beginnings of lyric poetry to Attic tragedy, breaks off all of a sudden immediately after attaining luxuriant development, and disappears, as it were, from the surface of Hellenic art: while the Dionysian view of things born of this striving lives on in Mysteries and, in its strangest metamorphoses and debasements, does not cease to attract earnest natures. Will it not one day rise again as art out of its mystic depth?

Here the question occupies us, whether the power by the counteracting influence of which tragedy perished, has for all time strength enough to prevent the artistic reawaking of tragedy and of the tragic view of things. If ancient tragedy was driven from its course by the dialectical desire for knowledge and the optimism of science, it might be inferred that there is an eternal conflict between *the theoretic* and *the tragic view of things,* and only after the spirit of science has been led to its boundaries, and its claim to universal validity has been destroyed by the evidence of these boundaries, can we hope for a re-birth of tragedy: for which form of culture we should have to use the symbol *of the music-practising Socrates* in the sense spoken of above. In this contrast, I understand by the spirit of science the belief which first came to light in the person of Socrates,—the belief in the fathomableness of nature and in knowledge as a panacea.

He who recalls the immediate consequences of this restlessly onward-pressing spirit of science will realise at once that *myth* was annihilated by it, and that, in consequence of this annihilation, poetry was driven as a homeless being from her natural ideal soil. If we have rightly assigned to music the capacity to reproduce myth from itself, we may in turn expect to find the spirit of science on the path where it inimically opposes this mythopoeic power of music. This takes place in the development of the *New Attic Dithyramb,* the music of which no longer expressed the inner essence, the will itself, but only rendered the phenomenon insufficiently, in an imitation by means of concepts; from which intrinsically degenerate music the truly musical natures turned away with the same repugnance that they felt for the art-destroying tendency of Socrates. The unerring instinct of Aristophanes surely did the proper thing when it comprised Socrates himself, the tragedy of Euripides, and the music of the new Dithyrambic poets in the same feeling of hatred, and perceived in all three phenomena the symptoms of a degenerate culture. By this New Dithyramb, music has in an outrageous manner been made the imitative portrait of phenomena, for instance, of a battle or a storm at sea, and has thus, of course, been entirely deprived of its mythopoeic power. For if it endeavours to excite our delight only by compelling us to seek external analogies between a vital or natural process and certain rhythmical figures and characteristic sounds of music; if our understanding is expected to satisfy itself with the perception of these analogies, we are reduced to a frame of mind in which the reception of the mythical is impossible; for the myth as a unique exemplar of generality and truth towering into the infinite, desires to be conspicuously perceived. The truly Dionysean music presents itself to us as such a general mirror of the universal will: the conspicuous event which is refracted in this mirror expands at once for our consciousness to the copy of an eternal truth. Conversely, such a conspicious event is at once divested of every mythical character by the tone-painting of the New Dithyramb; music has here become a wretched copy of the phenomenon, and therefore infinitely poorer than the phenomenon itself: through which poverty it still further reduces even the phenomenon for our consciousness, so that now, for instance, a musically imitated battle of this sort exhausts itself in marches, signal-sounds, etc., and our imagination is arrested precisely by these superficialities. Tone-painting is therefore in every respect the counterpart of true music with its mythopoeic power: through it the phenomenon, poor in itself, is made still poorer, while through an isolated Dionysian music the phenomenon is evolved and expanded into a picture of the world. It was an immense triumph of the non-Dionysian spirit, when, in the development of the New Dithyramb, it had estranged music from itself and reduced it to be the slave of phenomena. Euripides, who, albeit in a higher sense, must be designated as a thoroughly unmusical nature, is for this very reason a passionate adherent of the New Dithyrambic Music, and with the liberality of a freebooter employs all its effective turns and mannerisms.

In another direction also we see at work the power of this un-Dionysian, myth-opposing spirit, when we turn our eyes to the prevalence of *character representation* and psychological refinement from Sophocles onwards. The character must no longer be expanded into an eternal type, but, on the contrary, must operate individually through artistic by-traits and shadings, through the nicest precision of all lines, in such a manner that the spectator is in general no longer conscious of the myth, but of the mighty nature-myth and the imitative power of the artist. Here also we observe the victory of the phenomenon over the Universal, and the delight in the particular quasi-anatomical preparation; we actually breathe the air of a theoretical world, in which scientific knowledge is valued more highly than the artistic reflection of a universal law. The movement along the line of the representation of character proceeds rapidly: while Sophocles still delineates complete characters and employs myth for their refined development, Euripides already delineates only prominent individual traits of character, which can express themselves in violent bursts of passion; in the New Attic Comedy, however, there are only masks with *one* expression: frivolous old men, duped panders, and cunning slaves in untiring repetition. Where now is the mythopoeic spirit of music? What is still left now of music is either excitatory music or souvenir music, that is, either a stimulant for dull and used-up nerves, or tone-painting. As regards the former, it hardly matters about the text set to it: the heroes and choruses of Euripides are already dissolute enough when once they begin to sing; to what pass must things have come with his brazen successors?

The new un-Dionysian spirit, however, manifests itself most clearly in the *dénouements* of the new dramas. In the Old Tragedy one could feel at the close the metaphysical comfort, without which the delight in tragedy cannot be explained at all; the conciliating tones from another world sound purest, perhaps, in the Œdipus at Colonus. Now that the genius of music has fled from tragedy, tragedy is, strictly speaking, dead: for from whence could one now draw the metaphysical comfort? One sought, therefore, for an earthly unravelment of the tragic dissonance; the hero, after he had been sufficiently tortured by fate, reaped a well-deserved reward through a superb marriage or divine tokens of favour. The hero had turned gladiator, on whom, after being liberally battered about and covered with wounds, freedom was occasionally bestowed. The *deus ex machina* took the place of metaphysical comfort. I will not say that the tragic view of things was everywhere completely destroyed by the intruding spirit of the un-Dionysian: we only know that it was compelled to flee from art into the under-world as it were, in the degenerate form of a secret cult. Over the widest extent of the Hellenic character, however, there raged the consuming blast of this spirit, which manifests itself in the form of "Greek cheerfulness," which we have already spoken of as a senile, unproductive love of existence; this cheerfulness is the counterpart of the splendid "naïveté" of the earlier Greeks, which, according to the characteristic indicated above, must be conceived as the blossom of the Apollonian culture growing out of a dark abyss, as the victory which the Hellenic will, through its mirroring of beauty, obtains over suffering and the wisdom of suffering. The noblest manifestation of that other form of "Greek cheerfulness," the Alexandrine, is the cheerfulness of the *theoretical man*: it exhibits the same symptomatic characteristics as I have just inferred concerning the spirit of the un-Dionysian:—it combats Dionysian wisdom and art, it seeks to dissolve myth, it substitutes for metaphysical comfort an earthly consonance, in fact, a *deus ex machina*of its own, namely the god of machines and crucibles, that is, the powers of the genii of nature recognised and employed in the service of higher egoism; it believes in amending the world by knowledge, in guiding life by science, and that it can really confine the individual within a narrow sphere of solvable problems, where he cheerfully says to life: "I desire thee: it is worth while to know thee."

18.

It is an eternal phenomenon: the avidious will can always, by means of an illusion spread over things, detain its creatures in life and compel them to live on. One is chained by the Socratic love of knowledge and the vain hope of being able thereby to heal the eternal wound of existence; another is ensnared by art's seductive veil of beauty fluttering before his eyes; still another by the metaphysical comfort that eternal life flows on indestructibly beneath the whirl of phenomena: to say nothing of the more ordinary and almost more powerful illusions which the will has always at hand. These three specimens of illusion are on the whole designed only for the more nobly endowed natures, who in general feel profoundly the weight and burden of existence, and must be deluded into forgetfulness of their displeasure by exquisite stimulants. All that we call culture is made up of these stimulants; and, according to the proportion of the ingredients, we have either a specially *Socratic* or *artistic* or *tragic culture*: or, if historical exemplifications are wanted, there is either an Alexandrine or a Hellenic or a Buddhistic culture.

Our whole modern world is entangled in the meshes of Alexandrine culture, and recognises as its ideal the *theorist* equipped with the most potent means of knowledge, and labouring in the service of science, of whom the archetype and progenitor is Socrates. All our educational methods have originally this ideal in view: every other form of existence must struggle onwards wearisomely beside it, as something tolerated, but not intended. In an almost alarming manner the cultured man was here found for a long time only in the form of the scholar: even our poetical arts have been forced to evolve from learned imitations, and in the main effect of the rhyme we still recognise the origin of our poetic form from artistic experiments with a non-native and thoroughly learned language. How unintelligible must *Faust,* the modern cultured man, who is in himself intelligible, have appeared to a true Greek,—Faust, storming discontentedly through all the faculties, devoted to magic and the devil from a desire for knowledge, whom we have only to place alongside of Socrates for the purpose of comparison, in order to see that modern man begins to divine the boundaries of this Socratic love of perception and longs for a coast in the wide waste of the ocean of knowledge. When Goethe on one occasion said to Eckermann with reference to Napoleon: "Yes, my good friend, there is also a productiveness of deeds," he reminded us in a charmingly naïve manner that the non-theorist is something incredible and astounding to modern man; so that the wisdom of Goethe is needed once more in order to discover that such a surprising form of existence is comprehensible, nay even pardonable.

Now, we must not hide from ourselves what is concealed in the heart of this Socratic culture: Optimism, deeming itself absolute! Well, we must not be alarmed if the fruits of this optimism ripen,—if society, leavened to the very lowest strata by this kind of culture, gradually begins to tremble through wanton agitations and desires, if the belief in the earthly happiness of all, if the belief in the possibility of such a general intellectual culture is gradually transformed into the threatening demand for such an Alexandrine earthly happiness, into the conjuring of a Euripidean *deus ex machina.* Let us mark this well: the Alexandrine culture requires a slave class, to be able to exist permanently: but, in its optimistic view of life, it denies the necessity of such a class, and consequently, when the effect of its beautifully seductive and tranquillising utterances about the "dignity of man" and the "dignity of labour" is spent, it gradually drifts towards a dreadful destination. There is nothing more terrible than a barbaric slave class, who have learned to regard their existence as an injustice, and now prepare to take vengeance, not only for themselves, but for all generations. In the face of such threatening storms, who dares to appeal with confident spirit to our pale and exhausted religions, which even in their foundations have degenerated into scholastic religions?—so that myth, the necessary prerequisite of every religion, is already paralysed everywhere, and even in this domain the optimistic spirit—which we have just designated as the annihilating germ of society—has attained the mastery.

While the evil slumbering in the heart of theoretical culture gradually begins to disquiet modern man, and makes him anxiously ransack the stores of his experience for means to avert the danger, though not believing very much in these means; while he, therefore, begins to divine the consequences his position involves: great, universally gifted natures have contrived, with an incredible amount of thought, to make use of the apparatus of science itself, in order to point out the limits and the relativity of knowledge generally, and thus definitely to deny the claim of science to universal validity and universal ends: with which demonstration the illusory notion was for the first time recognised as such, which pretends, with the aid of causality, to be able to fathom the innermost essence of things. The extraordinary courage and wisdom of *Kant* and *Schopenhauer* have succeeded in gaining the most, difficult, victory, the victory over the optimism hidden in the essence of logic, which optimism in turn is the basis of our culture. While this optimism, resting on apparently unobjectionable *æterna veritates,* believed in the intelligibility and solvability of all the riddles of the world, and treated space, time, and causality as totally unconditioned laws of the most universal validity, Kant, on the other hand, showed that these served in reality only to elevate the mere phenomenon, the work of Mâyâ, to the sole and highest reality, putting it in place of the innermost and true essence of things, thus making the actual knowledge of this essence impossible, that is, according to the expression of Schopenhauer, to lull the dreamer still more soundly asleep (*Welt als Wille und Vorstellung,* I. 498). With this knowledge a culture is inaugurated which I venture to designate as a tragic culture; the most important characteristic of which is that wisdom takes the place of science as the highest end,—wisdom, which, uninfluenced by the seductive distractions of the sciences, turns with unmoved eye to the comprehensive view of the world, and seeks to apprehend therein the eternal suffering as its own with sympathetic feelings of love. Let us imagine a rising generation with this undauntedness of vision, with this heroic desire for the prodigious, let us imagine the bold step of these dragon-slayers, the proud and daring spirit with which they turn their backs on all the effeminate doctrines of optimism in order "to live resolutely" in the Whole and in the Full: would it not be necessary for the tragic man of this culture, with his self-discipline to earnestness and terror, to desire a new art, the art of metaphysical comfort,—namely, tragedy, as the Hellena belonging to him, and that he should exclaim with Faust:

Und sollt' ich nicht, sehnsüchtigster Gewalt,
In's Leben ziehn die einzigste Gestalt?*

But now that the Socratic culture has been shaken from two directions, and is only able to hold the sceptre of its infallibility with trembling hands,—once by the fear of its own conclusions which it at length begins to surmise, and again, because it is no longer convinced with its former naïve trust of the eternal validity of its foundation, —it is a sad spectacle to behold how the dance of its thought always rushes longingly on new forms, to embrace them, and then, shuddering, lets them go of a sudden, as Mephistopheles does the seductive Lamiæ. It is certainly the symptom of the "breach" which all are wont to speak of as the primordial suffering of modern culture that the theoretical man, alarmed and dissatisfied at his own conclusions, no longer dares to entrust himself to the terrible ice-stream of existence: he runs timidly up and down the bank. He no longer wants to have anything entire, with all the natural cruelty of things, so thoroughly has he been spoiled by his optimistic contemplation. Besides, he feels that a culture built up on the principles of science must perish when it begins to grow *illogical,* that is, to avoid its own conclusions. Our art reveals this universal trouble: in vain does one seek help by imitating all the great productive periods and natures, in vain does one accumulate the entire "world-literature" around modern man for his comfort, in vain does one place one's self in the midst of the art-styles and artists of all ages, so that one may give names to them as Adam did to the beasts: one still continues the eternal hungerer, the "critic" without joy and energy, the Alexandrine man, who is in the main a librarian and corrector of proofs, and who, pitiable wretch goes blind from the dust of books and printers' errors.

19.

We cannot designate the intrinsic substance of Socratic culture more distinctly than by calling it *the culture of the opera*: for it is in this department that culture has expressed itself with special naïveté concerning its aims and perceptions, which is sufficiently surprising when we compare the genesis of the opera and the facts of operatic development with the eternal truths of the Apollonian and Dionysian. I call to mind first of all the origin of the *stilo rappresentativo* and the recitative. Is it credible that this thoroughly externalised operatic music, incapable of devotion, could be received and cherished with enthusiastic favour, as a re-birth, as it were, of all true music, by the very age

* Cf. Introduction, p. 14.

in which the ineffably sublime and sacred music of Palestrina had originated? And who, on the other hand, would think of making only the diversion-craving luxuriousness of those Florentine circles and the vanity of their dramatic singers responsible for the love of the opera which spread with such rapidity? That in the same age, even among the same people, this passion for a half-musical mode of speech should awaken alongside of the vaulted structure of Palestrine harmonies which the entire Christian Middle Age had been building up, I can explain to myself only by a co-operating *extra-artistic tendency* in the essence of the recitative.

The listener, who insists on distinctly hearing the words under the music, has his wishes met by the singer in that he speaks rather than sings, and intensifies the pathetic expression of the words in this half-song: by this intensification of the pathos he facilitates the understanding of the words and surmounts the remaining half of the music. The specific danger which now threatens him is that in some unguarded moment he may give undue importance to music, which would forthwith result in the destruction of the pathos of the speech and the distinctness of the words: while, on the other hand, he always feels himself impelled to musical delivery and to virtuose exhibition of vocal talent. Here the "poet" comes to his aid, who knows how to provide him with abundant opportunities for lyrical interjections, repetitions of words and sentences, etc.,—at which places the singer, now in the purely musical element, can rest himself without minding the words. This alternation of emotionally impressive, yet only half-sung speech and wholly sung interjections, which is characteristic of the *stilo rappresentativo,* this rapidly changing endeavour to operate now on the conceptional and representative faculty of the hearer, now on his musical sense, is something so thoroughly unnatural and withal so intrinsically contradictory both to the Apollonian and Dionysian artistic impulses, that one has to infer an origin of the recitative foreign to all artistic instincts. The recitative must be defined, according to this description, as the combination of epic and lyric delivery, not indeed as an intrinsically stable combination which could not be attained in the case of such totally disparate elements, but an entirely superficial mosaic conglutination, such as is totally unprecedented in the domain of nature and experience. *But this was not the opinion of the inventors of the recitative:* they themselves, and their age with them, believed rather that the mystery of antique music had been solved by this *stilo rappresentativo,* in which, as they thought, the only explanation of the enormous influence of an Orpheus, an Amphion, and even of Greek tragedy was to be found. The new style was regarded by them as the re-awakening of the most effective music, the Old Greek music: indeed, with the universal and popular conception of the Homeric world *as the primitive world,* they could abandon themselves to the dream of having descended once more into the paradisiac beginnings of mankind, wherein music also must needs have had the unsurpassed purity, power, and innocence of which the poets could give such touching accounts in their pastoral plays. Here we see into the internal process of development of this thoroughly modern variety of art, the opera: a powerful need here acquires an art, but it is a need of an unæsthetic kind: the yearning for the idyll, the belief in the prehistoric existence of the artistic, good man. The recitative was regarded as the rediscovered language of this primitive man; the opera as the recovered land of this idyllically or heroically good creature, who in every action follows at the same time a natural artistic impulse, who sings a little along with all he has to say, in order to sing immediately with full voice on the slightest emotional excitement. It is now a matter of indifference to us that the humanists of those days combated the old ecclesiastical representation of man as naturally corrupt and lost, with this new-created picture of the paradisiac artist: so that opera may be understood as the oppositional dogma of the good man, whereby however a solace was at the same time found for the pessimism to which precisely the seriously-disposed men of that time were most strongly incited, owing to the frightful uncertainty of all conditions of life. It is enough to have perceived that the intrinsic charm, and therefore the genesis, of this new form of art lies in the gratification of an altogether unæsthetic need, in the optimistic glorification of man as such, in the conception of the primitive man as the man naturally good and artistic: a principle of the opera which has gradually changed into a threatening and terrible *demand,* which, in face of the socialistic movements of the present time, we can no longer ignore. The "good primitive man" wants his rights: what paradisiac prospects!

I here place by way of parallel still another equally obvious confirmation of my view that opera is built up on the same principles as our Alexandrine culture. Opera is the birth of the theoretical man, of the critical layman, not of the artist: one of the most surprising facts in the whole history of art. It was the demand of thoroughly unmusical hearers that the words must above all be understood, so that according to them a re-birth of music is only to be expected when some mode of singing has been discovered in which the text-word lords over the counterpoint as the master over the servant. For the words, it is argued, are as much nobler than the accompanying harmonic system as the soul is nobler than the body. It was in accordance with the laically unmusical crudeness of these views that the combination of music, picture and expression was effected in the beginnings of the opera: in the spirit of this æsthetics the first experiments were also made in the leading laic circles of Florence by the poets and singers patronised there. The man incapable of art creates for himself a species of art precisely because he is the inartistic man as such. Because he does not divine the Dionysian depth of music, he changes his musical taste into appreciation of the understandable word-and-tone-rhetoric of the passions in the *stilo rappresentativo,* and into the voluptuousness of the arts of song; because he is unable to behold a vision, he forces the machinist and the decorative artist into his service; because he cannot apprehend the true nature of the artist, he conjures up the "artistic primitive man" to suit his taste, that is, the man who sings and recites verses under the influence of passion. He dreams himself into a time when passion suffices to generate songs and poems: as if emotion had ever been able to create anything artistic. The postulate of the opera is a false belief concerning the artistic process, in fact, the idyllic belief that every sentient man is an artist. In the sense of this belief, opera is the expression of the taste of the laity in art, who dictate their laws with the cheerful optimism of the theorist.

Should we desire to unite in one the two conceptions just set forth as influential in the origin of opera, it would only remain for us to speak of an *idyllic tendency of the opera*: in which connection we may avail ourselves exclusively of the phraseology and illustration of Schiller.* "Nature and the ideal," he says, "are either objects of grief, when the former is represented as lost, the latter unattained; or both are objects of joy, in that they are represented as real. The first case furnishes the elegy in its narrower signification, the second the idyll in its widest sense." Here we must at once call attention to the common characteristic of these two conceptions in operatic genesis, namely, that in them the ideal is not regarded as unattained or nature as lost Agreeably to this sentiment, there was a primitive age of man when he lay close to the heart of nature, and, owing to this naturalness, had attained the ideal of mankind in a paradisiac goodness and artist-organisation: from which perfect primitive man all of us were supposed to be descended; whose faithful copy we were in fact still said to be: only we had to cast off some few things in order to recognise ourselves once more as this primitive man, on the strength of a voluntary renunciation of superfluous learnedness, of super-abundant culture. It was to such a concord of nature and the ideal, to an idyllic reality, that the cultured man of the Renaissance suffered himself to be led back by his operatic imitation of Greek tragedy; he made use of this tragedy, as Dante made use of Vergil, in order to be led up to the gates of paradise: while from this point he went on without assistance and passed over from an imitation of the highest form of Greek art to a "restoration of all things," to an imitation of man's original art-world. What delightfully naïve hopefulness of these daring endeavours, in the very heart of theoretical culture!—solely to be explained by the comforting belief, that "man-in-himself" is the eternally virtuous hero of the opera, the eternally fluting or singing shepherd, who must always in the end rediscover himself as such, if he has at any time really lost himself; solely the fruit of the optimism, which here rises like a sweetishly seductive column of vapour out of the depth of the Socratic conception of the world.

The features of the opera therefore do not by any means exhibit the elegiac sorrow of an eternal loss, but rather the cheerfulness of eternal rediscovery,

* Essay on Elegiac Poetry.—TR.

the indolent delight in an idyllic reality which one can at least represent to one's self each moment as real: and in so doing one will perhaps surmise some day that this supposed reality is nothing but a fantastically silly dawdling, concerning which every one, who could judge it by the terrible earnestness of true nature and compare it with the actual primitive scenes of the beginnings of mankind, would have to call out with loathing: Away with the phantom! Nevertheless one would err if one thought it possible to frighten away merely by a vigorous shout such a dawdling thing as the opera, as if it were a spectre. He who would destroy the opera must join issue with Alexandrine cheerfulness, which expresses itself so naïvely therein concerning its favourite representation; of which in fact it is the specific form of art. But what is to be expected for art itself from the operation of a form of art, the beginnings of which do not at all lie in the æsthetic province; which has rather stolen over from a half-moral sphere into the artistic domain, and has been able only now and then to delude us concerning this hybrid origin? By what sap is this parasitic opera-concern nourished, if not by that of true art? Must we not suppose that the highest and indeed the truly serious task of art—to free the eye from its glance into the horrors of night and to deliver the "subject" by the healing balm of appearance from the spasms of volitional agitations—will degenerate under the influence of its idyllic seductions and Alexandrine adulation to an empty dissipating tendency, to pastime? What will become of the eternal truths of the Dionysian and Apollonian in such an amalgamation of styles as I have exhibited in the character of the *stilo rappresentativo*? where music is regarded as the servant, the text as the master, where music is compared with the body, the text with the soul? where at best the highest aim will be the realisation of a paraphrastic tone-painting, just as formerly in the New Attic Dithyramb? where music is completely alienated from its true dignity of being, the Dionysian mirror of the world, so that the only thing left to it is, as a slave of phenomena, to imitate the formal character thereof, and to excite an external pleasure in the play of lines and proportions. On close observation, this fatal influence of the opera on music is seen to coincide absolutely with the universal development of modern music; the optimism lurking in the genesis of the opera and in the essence of culture represented thereby, has, with alarming rapidity, succeeded in divesting music of its Dionyso-cosmic mission and in impressing on it a playfully formal and pleasurable character: a change with which perhaps only the metamorphosis of the Æschylean man into the cheerful Alexandrine man could be compared.

If, however, in the exemplification herewith indicated we have rightly associated the evanescence of the Dionysian spirit with a most striking, but hitherto unexplained transformation and degeneration of the Hellene—what hopes must revive in us when the most trustworthy auspices guarantee *the reverse process, the gradual awakening of the Dionysian spirit* in our modern world! It is impossible for the divine strength of Herakles to languish for ever in voluptuous bondage to Omphale. Out of the Dionysian root of the German spirit a power has arisen which has nothing in common with the primitive conditions of Socratic culture, and can neither be explained nor excused thereby, but is rather regarded by this culture as something terribly inexplicable and overwhelmingly hostile,mdash;namely, *German music* as we have to understand it, especially in its vast solar orbit from Bach to Beethoven, from Beethoven to Wagner. What even under the most favourable circumstances can the knowledge-craving Socratism of our days do with this demon rising from unfathomable depths? Neither by means of the zig-zag and arabesque work of operatic melody, nor with the aid of the arithmetical counting board of fugue and contrapuntal dialectics is the formula to be found, in the trebly powerful light* of which one could subdue this demon and compel it to speak. What a spectacle, when our æsthetes, with a net of "beauty" peculiar to themselves, now pursue and clutch at the genius of music romping about before them with incomprehensible life, and in so doing display activities which are not to be judged by the standard of eternal beauty any more than by the standard of the sublime. Let us but observe these patrons of music as they are, at close range, when they call out so indefatigably "beauty! beauty!" to discover whether they have the marks of nature's darling children who are fostered and fondled in the lap of the beautiful, or whether they do not rather seek a disguise for their own rudeness, an æsthetical pretext for their own unemotional insipidity: I am thinking here, for instance, of Otto Jahn. But let the liar and the hypocrite beware of our German music: for in the midst of all our culture it is really the only genuine, pure and purifying fire-spirit from which and towards which, as in the teaching of the great Heraclitus of Ephesus, all things move in a double orbit-all that we now call culture, education, civilisation, must appear some day before the unerring judge, Dionysus.

Let us recollect furthermore how Kant and Schopenhauer made it possible for the spirit of *German philosophy* streaming from the same sources to annihilate the satisfied delight in existence of scientific Socratism by the delimitation of the boundaries thereof; how through this delimitation an infinitely profounder and more serious view of ethical problems and of art was inaugurated, which we may unhesitatingly designate as *Dionysian* wisdom comprised in concepts. To what then does the mystery of this oneness of German music and philosophy point, if not to a new form of existence, concerning the substance of which we can only inform ourselves presentiently from Hellenic analogies? For to us who stand on the boundary line between two different forms of existence, the Hellenic prototype retains the immeasurable value, that therein all these transitions and struggles are imprinted in a classically instructive form: except that we, as it were, experience analogically in *reverse* order the chief epochs of the Hellenic genius, and seem now, for instance, to

---

* See *Faust,* Part 1.1. 965—TR.

pass backwards from the Alexandrine age to the period of tragedy. At the same time we have the feeling that the birth of a tragic age betokens only a return to itself of the German spirit, a blessed self-rediscovering after excessive and urgent external influences have for a long time compelled it, living as it did in helpless barbaric formlessness, to servitude under their form. It may at last, after returning to the primitive source of its being, venture to stalk along boldly and freely before all nations without hugging the leading-strings of a Romanic civilisation: if only it can learn implicitly of one people—the Greeks, of whom to learn at all is itself a high honour and a rare distinction. And when did we require these highest of all teachers more than at present, when we experience *a re-birth of tragedy* and are in danger alike of not knowing whence it comes, and of being unable to make clear to ourselves whither it tends.

20.

It may be weighed some day before an impartial judge, in what time and in what men the German spirit has thus far striven most resolutely to learn of the Greeks: and if we confidently assume that this unique praise must be accorded to the noblest intellectual efforts of Goethe, Schiller, and Winkelmann, it will certainly have to be added that since their time, and subsequently to the more immediate influences of these efforts, the endeavour to attain to culture and to the Greeks by this path has in an incomprehensible manner grown feebler and feebler. In order not to despair altogether of the German spirit, must we not infer therefrom that possibly, in some essential matter, even these champions could not penetrate into the core of the Hellenic nature, and were unable to establish a permanent friendly alliance between German and Greek culture? So that perhaps an unconscious perception of this shortcoming might raise also in more serious minds the disheartening doubt as to whether after such predecessors they could advance still farther on this path of culture, or could reach the goal at all. Accordingly, we see the opinions concerning the value of Greek contribution to culture degenerate since that time in the most alarming manner; the expression of compassionate superiority may be heard in the most heterogeneous intellectual and non-intellectual camps, and elsewhere a totally ineffective declamation dallies with "Greek harmony," "Greek beauty," "Greek cheerfulness." And in the very circles whose dignity it might be to draw indefatigably from the Greek channel for the good of German culture, in the circles of the teachers in the higher educational institutions, they have learned best to compromise with the Greeks in good time and on easy terms, to the extent often of a sceptical abandonment of the Hellenic ideal and a total perversion of the true purpose of antiquarian studies. If there be any one at all in these circles who has not completely exhausted himself in the endeavour to be a trustworthy corrector of old texts or a natural-history microscopist of language, he perhaps seeks also to appropriate Grecian antiquity "historically" along with other antiquities, and in any case according to the method and with the supercilious air of our present cultured historiography. When, therefore, the intrinsic efficiency of the higher educational institutions has never perhaps been lower or feebler than at present, when the "journalist," the paper slave of the day, has triumphed over the academic teacher in all matters pertaining to culture, and there only remains to the latter the often previously experienced metamorphosis of now fluttering also, as a cheerful cultured butterfly, in the idiom of the journalist, with the "light elegance" peculiar thereto—with what painful confusion must the cultured persons of a period like the present gaze at the phenomenon (which can perhaps be comprehended analogically only by means of the profoundest principle of the hitherto unintelligible Hellenic genius) of the reawakening of the Dionysian spirit and the re-birth of tragedy? Never has there been another art-period in which so-called culture and true art have been so estranged and opposed, as is so obviously the case at present. We understand why so feeble a culture hates true art; it fears destruction thereby. But must not an entire domain of culture, namely the Socratic-Alexandrine, have exhausted its powers after contriving to culminate in such a daintily-tapering point as our present culture? When it was not permitted to heroes like Goethe and Schiller to break open the enchanted gate which leads into the Hellenic magic mountain, when with their most dauntless striving they did not get beyond the longing gaze which the Goethean Iphigenia cast from barbaric Tauris to her home across the ocean, what could the epigones of such heroes hope for, if the gate should not open to them suddenly of its own accord, in an entirely different position, quite overlooked in all endeavours of culture hitherto—amidst the mystic tones of reawakened tragic music.

Let no one attempt to weaken our faith in an impending re-birth of Hellenic antiquity; for in it alone we find our hope of a renovation and purification of the German spirit through the fire-magic of music. What else do we know of amidst the present desolation and languor of culture, which could awaken any comforting expectation for the future? We look in vain for one single vigorously-branching root, for a speck of fertile and healthy soil: there is dust, sand, torpidness and languishing everywhere! Under such circumstances a cheerless solitary wanderer could choose for himself no better symbol than the Knight with Death and the Devil, as Dürer has sketched him for us, the mail-clad knight, grim and stern of visage, who is able, unperturbed by his gruesome companions, and yet hopelessly, to pursue his terrible path with horse and hound alone. Our Schopenhauer was such a Dürerian knight: he was destitute of all hope, but he sought the truth. There is not his equal.

But how suddenly this gloomily depicted wilderness of our exhausted culture changes when the Dionysian magic touches it! A hurricane seizes everything decrepit, decaying, collapsed, and stunted; wraps it whirlingly into a red cloud of dust; and carries it like a vulture into the air. Confused thereby, our glances seek for what has vanished: for what they see is something risen to the golden light as from a depression, so full and green, so luxuriantly alive, so ardently infinite. Tragedy sits in the midst of this exuberance of life, sorrow and joy, in sublime ecstasy; she listens to a distant doleful song—it tells of the Mothers of Being, whose names are: *Wahn, Wille, Wehe**—Yes, my friends, believe with me in Dionysian life and in the re-birth of tragedy. The time of the Socratic man is past: crown yourselves with ivy, take in your hands the thyrsus, and do not marvel if tigers and panthers lie down fawning at your feet. Dare now to be tragic men, for ye are to be redeemed! Ye are to accompany the Dionysian festive procession from India to Greece! Equip yourselves for severe conflict, but believe in the wonders of your god!

21.

Gliding back from these hortative tones into the mood which befits the contemplative man, I repeat that it can only be learnt from the Greeks what such a sudden and miraculous awakening of tragedy must signify for the essential basis of a people's life. It is the people of the tragic mysteries who fight the battles with the Persians: and again, the people who waged such wars required tragedy as a necessary healing potion. Who would have imagined that there was still such a uniformly powerful effusion of the simplest political sentiments, the most natural domestic instincts and the primitive manly delight in strife in this very people after it had been shaken to its foundations for several generations by the most violent convulsions of the Dionysian demon? If at every considerable spreading of the Dionysian commotion one always perceives that the Dionysian loosing from the shackles of the individual makes itself felt first of all in an increased encroachment on the political instincts, to the extent of indifference, yea even hostility, it is certain, on the other hand, that the state-forming Apollo is also the genius of the *principium individuationis,* and that the state and domestic sentiment cannot live without an assertion of individual personality. There is only one way from orgasm for a people,—the way to Indian Buddhism, which, in order to be at all endured with its longing for nothingness, requires the rare ecstatic states with their elevation above space, time, and the individual; just as these in turn demand a philosophy which teaches how to overcome the indescribable depression of the intermediate states by means of a fancy. With the same necessity, owing to the unconditional dominance of political impulses, a people drifts into a path of extremest secularisation, the most magnificent, but also the most terrible expression of which is the Roman *imperium.*

Placed between India and Rome, and constrained to a seductive choice, the Greeks succeeded in devising in classical purity still a third form of life,

* Whim, will woe.

not indeed for long private use, but just on that account for immortality. For it holds true in all things that those whom the gods love die young, but, on the other hand, it holds equally true that they then live eternally with the gods. One must not demand of what is most noble that it should possess the durable toughness of leather; the staunch durability, which, for instance, was inherent in the national character of the Romans, does not probably belong to the indispensable predicates of perfection. But if we ask by what physic it was possible for the Greeks, in their best period, notwithstanding the extraordinary strength of their Dionysian and political impulses, neither to exhaust themselves by ecstatic brooding, nor by a consuming scramble for empire and worldly honour, but to attain the splendid mixture which we find in a noble, inflaming, and contemplatively disposing wine, we must remember the enormous power of *tragedy,* exciting, purifying, and disburdening the entire life of a people; the highest value of which we shall divine only when, as in the case of the Greeks, it appears to us as the essence of all the prophylactic healing forces, as the mediator arbitrating between the strongest and most inherently fateful characteristics of a people.

Tragedy absorbs the highest musical orgasm into itself, so that it absolutely brings music to perfection among the Greeks, as among ourselves; but it then places alongside thereof tragic myth and the tragic hero, who, like a mighty Titan, takes the entire Dionysian world on his shoulders and disburdens us thereof; while, on the other hand, it is able by means of this same tragic myth, in the person of the tragic hero, to deliver us from the intense longing for this existence, and reminds us with warning hand of another existence and a higher joy, for which the struggling hero prepares himself presentiently by his destruction, not by his victories. Tragedy sets a sublime symbol, namely the myth between the universal authority of its music and the receptive Dionysian hearer, and produces in him the illusion that music is only the most effective means for the animation of the plastic world of myth. Relying upon this noble illusion, she can now move her limbs for the dithyrambic dance, and abandon herself unhesitatingly to an orgiastic feeling of freedom, in which she could not venture to indulge as music itself, without this illusion. The myth protects us from the music, while, on the other hand, it alone gives the highest freedom thereto. By way of return for this service, music imparts to tragic myth such an impressive and convincing metaphysical significance as could never be attained by word and image, without this unique aid; and the tragic spectator in particular experiences thereby the sure presentiment of supreme joy to which the path through destruction and negation leads; so that he thinks he hears, as it were, the innermost abyss of things speaking audibly to him.

If in these last propositions I have succeeded in giving perhaps only a preliminary expression, intelligible to few at first, to this difficult representation, I must not here desist from stimulating my friends to a further attempt, or cease from beseeching them to prepare themselves, by a detached example of our common experience, for the perception of the universal proposition. In this example I must not appeal to those who make use of the pictures of the scenic processes, the words and the emotions of the performers, in order to approximate thereby to musical perception; for none of these speak music as their mother-tongue, and, in spite of the aids in question, do not get farther than the precincts of musical perception, without ever being allowed to touch its innermost shrines; some of them, like Gervinus, do not even reach the precincts by this path. I have only to address myself to those who, being immediately allied to music, have it as it were for their mother's lap, and are connected with things almost exclusively by unconscious musical relations. I ask the question of these genuine musicians: whether they can imagine a man capable of hearing the third act of *Tristan und Isolde* without any aid of word or scenery, purely as a vast symphonic period, without expiring by a spasmodic distention of all the wings of the soul? A man who has thus, so to speak, put his ear to the heart-chamber of the cosmic will, who feels the furious desire for existence issuing therefrom as a thundering stream or most gently dispersed brook, into all the veins of the world, would he not collapse all at once? Could he endure, in the wretched fragile tenement of the human individual, to hear the re-echo of countless cries of joy and sorrow from the "vast void of cosmic night," without flying irresistibly towards his primitive home at the sound of this pastoral dance-song of metaphysics? But if, nevertheless, such a work can be heard as a whole, without a renunciation of individual existence, if such a creation could be created without demolishing its creator—where are we to get the solution of this contradiction?

Here there interpose between our highest musical excitement and the music in question the tragic myth and the tragic hero—in reality only as symbols of the most universal facts, of which music alone can speak directly. If, however, we felt as purely Dionysian beings, myth as a symbol would stand by us absolutely ineffective and unnoticed, and would never for a moment prevent us from giving ear to the re-echo of the *universalia ante rem*. Here, however, the *Apollonian* power, with a view to the restoration of the well-nigh shattered individual, bursts forth with the healing balm of a blissful illusion: all of a sudden we imagine we see only Tristan, motionless, with hushed voice saying to himself: "the old tune, why does it wake me?" And what formerly interested us like a hollow sigh from the heart of being, seems now only to tell us how "waste and void is the sea." And when, breathless, we thought to expire by a convulsive distention of all our feelings, and only a slender tie bound us to our present existence, we now hear and see only the hero wounded to death and still not dying, with his despairing cry: "Longing! Longing! In dying still longing! for longing not dying!" And if formerly, after such a surplus and superabundance of consuming agonies, the jubilation of the born rent our hearts almost like the very acme of agony, the rejoicing Kurwenal now stands between us and the "jubilation as such," with face turned toward the ship which carries Isolde. However powerfully fellow-suffering encroaches upon us, it nevertheless delivers us in a manner from the primordial suffering of the world, just as the symbol-image of the myth delivers us from the immediate perception of the highest cosmic idea, just as the thought and word deliver us from the unchecked effusion of the unconscious will. The glorious Apollonian illusion makes it appear as if the very realm of tones presented itself to us as a plastic cosmos, as if even the fate of Tristan and Isolde had been merely formed and moulded therein as out of some most delicate and impressible material.

Thus does the Apollonian wrest us from Dionysian universality and fill us with rapture for individuals; to these it rivets our sympathetic emotion, through these it satisfies the sense of beauty which longs for great and sublime forms; it brings before us biographical portraits, and incites us to a thoughtful apprehension of the essence of life contained therein. With the immense potency of the image, the concept, the ethical teaching and the sympathetic emotion—the Apollonian influence uplifts man from his orgiastic self-annihilation, and beguiles him concerning the universality of the Dionysian process into the belief that he is seeing a detached picture of the world, for instance, Tristan and Isolde, and that, *through music,* he will be enabled to *see* it still more clearly and intrinsically. What can the healing magic of Apollo not accomplish when it can even excite in us the illusion that the Dionysian is actually in the service of the Apollonian, the effects of which it is capable of enhancing; yea, that music is essentially the representative art for an Apollonian substance?

With the pre-established harmony which obtains between perfect drama and its music, the drama attains the highest degree of conspicuousness, such as is usually unattainable in mere spoken drama. As all the animated figures of the scene in the independently evolved lines of melody simplify themselves before us to the distinctness of the catenary curve, the coexistence of these lines is also audible in the harmonic change which sympathises in a most delicate manner with the evolved process: through which change the relations of things become immediately perceptible to us in a sensible and not at all abstract manner, as we likewise perceive thereby that it is only in these relations that the essence of a character and of a line of melody manifests itself clearly. And while music thus compels us to see more extensively and more intrinsically than usual, and makes us spread out the curtain of the scene before ourselves like some delicate texture, the world of the stage is as infinitely expanded for our spiritualised, introspective eye as it is illumined outwardly from within. How can the word-poet furnish anything analogous, who strives to attain this internal expansion and illumination of the visible stage-world by a much more imperfect mechanism and an indirect path, proceeding as he does from word and concept? Albeit musical tragedy likewise avails itself of the word, it is at the same time able to place alongside thereof its basis and source, and can make the unfolding of the word, from within outwards, obvious to us.

Of the process just set forth, however, it could still be said as decidedly that it is only a glorious appearance, namely the afore-mentioned Apollonian *illusion,* through the influence of which we are to be delivered from the Dionysian obtrusion and excess. In point of fact, the relation of music to drama is precisely the reverse; music is the adequate idea of the world, drama is but the reflex of this idea, a detached umbrage thereof. The identity between the line of melody and the lining form, between the harmony and the character-relations of this form, is true in a sense antithetical to what one would suppose on the contemplation of musical tragedy. We may agitate and enliven the form in the most conspicuous manner, and enlighten it from within, but it still continues merely phenomenon, from which there is no bridge to lead us into the true reality, into the heart of the world. Music, however, speaks out of this heart; and though countless phenomena of the kind might be passing manifestations of this music, they could never exhaust its essence, but would always be merely its externalised copies. Of course, as regards the intricate relation of music and drama, nothing can be explained, while all may be confused by the popular and thoroughly false antithesis of soul and body; but the unphilosophical crudeness of this antithesis seems to have become—who knows for what reasons—a readily accepted Article of Faith with our æstheticians, while they have learned nothing concerning an antithesis of phenomenon and thing-in-itself, or perhaps, for reasons equally unknown, have not cared to learn anything thereof.

Should it have been established by our analysis that the Apollonian element in tragedy has by means of its illusion gained a complete victory over the Dionysian primordial element of music, and has made music itself subservient to its end, namely, the highest and clearest elucidation of the drama, it would certainly be necessary to add the very important restriction: that at the most essential point this Apollonian illusion is dissolved and annihilated. The drama, which, by the aid of music, spreads out before us with such inwardly illumined distinctness in all its movements and figures, that we imagine we see the texture unfolding on the loom as the shuttle flies to and fro,—attains as a whole an effect which *transcends all Apollonian artistic effects.* In the collective effect of tragedy, the Dionysian gets the upper hand once more; tragedy ends with a sound which could never emanate from the realm of Apollonian art. And the Apollonian illusion is thereby found to be what it is,—the assiduous veiling during the performance of tragedy of the intrinsically Dionysian effect: which, however, is so powerful, that it finally forces the Apollonian drama itself into a sphere where it begins to talk with Dionysian wisdom, and even denies itself and its Apollonian conspicuousness. Thus then the intricate relation of the Apollonian and the Dionysian in tragedy must really be symbolised by a fraternal union of the two deities: Dionysus speaks the language of Apollo; Apollo, however, finally speaks the language of Dionysus; and so the highest goal of tragedy and of art in general is attained.

22.

Let the attentive friend picture to himself purely and simply, according to his experiences, the effect of a true musical tragedy. I think I have so portrayed the phenomenon of this effect in both its phases that he will now be able to interpret his own experiences. For he will recollect that with regard to the myth which passed before him he felt himself exalted to a kind of omniscience, as if his visual faculty were no longer merely a surface faculty, but capable of penetrating into the interior, and as if he now saw before him, with the aid of music, the ebullitions of the will, the conflict of motives, and the swelling stream of the passions, almost sensibly visible, like a plenitude of actively moving lines and figures, and could thereby dip into the most tender secrets of unconscious emotions. While he thus becomes conscious of the highest exaltation of his instincts for conspicuousness and transfiguration, he nevertheless feels with equal definitiveness that this long series of Apollonian artistic effects still does *not* generate the blissful continuance in will-less contemplation which the plasticist and the epic poet, that is to say, the strictly Apollonian artists, produce in him by their artistic productions: to wit, the justification of the world of the *individuatio* attained in this contemplation,—which is the object and essence of Apollonian art. He beholds the transfigured world of the stage and nevertheless denies it. He sees before him the tragic hero in epic clearness and beauty, and nevertheless delights in his annihilation. He comprehends the incidents of the scene in all their details, and yet loves to flee into the incomprehensible. He feels the actions of the hero to be justified, and is nevertheless still more elated when these actions annihilate their originator. He shudders at the sufferings which will befall the hero, and yet anticipates therein a higher and much more overpowering joy. He sees more extensively and profoundly than ever, and yet wishes to be blind. Whence must we derive this curious internal dissension, this collapse of the Apollonian apex, if not from the *Dionysian* spell, which, though apparently stimulating the Apollonian emotions to their highest pitch, can nevertheless force this superabundance of Apollonian power into its service? *Tragic myth* is to be understood only as a symbolisation of Dionysian wisdom by means of the expedients of Apollonian art: the mythus conducts the world of phenomena to its boundaries, where it denies itself, and seeks to flee back again into the bosom of the true and only reality; where it then, like Isolde, seems to strike up its metaphysical swan-song:—

In des Wonnemeeres
wogendem Schwall,
in der Duft-Wellen
tönendem Schall,
in des Weltathems
wehendem All—

ertrinken—versinken
unbewusst—höchste Lust!*

We thus realise to ourselves in the experiences of the truly æsthetic hearer the tragic artist himself when he proceeds like a luxuriously fertile divinity of individuation to create his figures (in which sense his work can hardly be understood as an "imitation of nature")—and when, on the other hand, his vast Dionysian impulse then absorbs the entire world of phenomena, in order to anticipate beyond it, and through its annihilation, the highest artistic primal joy, in the bosom of the Primordial Unity. Of course, our æsthetes have nothing to say about this return in fraternal union of the two art-deities to the original home, nor of either the Apollonian or Dionysian excitement of the hearer, while they are indefatigable in characterising the struggle of the hero with fate, the triumph of the moral order of the world, or the disburdenment of the emotions through tragedy, as the properly Tragic: an indefatigableness which makes me think that they are perhaps not æsthetically excitable men at all, but only to be regarded as moral beings when hearing tragedy. Never since Aristotle has an explanation of the tragic effect been proposed, by which an æsthetic activity of the hearer could be inferred from artistic circumstances. At one time fear and pity are supposed to be forced to an alleviating discharge through the serious procedure, at another time we are expected to feel elevated and inspired at the triumph of good and noble principles, at the sacrifice of the hero in the interest of a moral conception of things; and however certainly I believe that for countless men precisely this, and only this, is the effect of tragedy, it as obviously follows therefrom that all these, together with their interpreting æsthetes, have had no experience of tragedy as the highest *art*. The pathological discharge, the catharsis of Aristotle, which philologists are at a loss whether to include under medicinal or moral phenomena, recalls a remarkable anticipation of Goethe. "Without a lively pathological interest," he says, "I too have never yet succeeded in elaborating a tragic situation of any kind, and hence I have rather avoided than sought it. Can it perhaps have been still another of the merits of the ancients that the deepest pathos was with them merely æsthetic play, whereas with us the truth of nature must co-operate in order to produce such a work?" We can now answer in the affirmative this latter profound question after our glorious experiences, in which we have found to our astonishment in the case of musical tragedy itself, that the deepest pathos

* In the sea of pleasure's
Billowing roll,
In the ether-waves
Knelling and toll,
In the world-breath's
Wavering whole—
To drown in, go down in—
Lost in swoon—greatest boon!

can in reality be merely æsthetic play: and therefore we are justified in believing that now for the first time the proto-phenomenon of the tragic can be portrayed with some degree of success. He who now will still persist in talking only of those vicarious effects proceeding from ultra-æsthetic spheres, and does not feel himself raised above the pathologically-moral process, may be left to despair of his æsthetic nature: for which we recommend to him, by way of innocent equivalent, the interpretation of Shakespeare after the fashion of Gervinus, and the diligent search for poetic justice.

Thus with the re-birth of tragedy the *æsthetic hearer* is also born anew, in whose place in the theatre a curious *quid pro quo* was wont to sit with half-moral and half-learned pretensions,—the "critic." In his sphere hitherto everything has been artificial and merely glossed over with a semblance of life. The performing artist was in fact at a loss what to do with such a critically comporting hearer, and hence he, as well as the dramatist or operatic composer who inspired him, searched anxiously for the last remains of life in a being so pretentiously barren and incapable of enjoyment. Such "critics," however, have hitherto constituted the public; the student, the school-boy, yea, even the most harmless womanly creature, were already unwittingly prepared by education and by journals for a similar perception of works of art. The nobler natures among the artists counted upon exciting the moral-religious forces in such a public, and the appeal to a moral order of the world operated vicariously, when in reality some powerful artistic spell should have enraptured the true hearer. Or again, some imposing or at all events exciting tendency of the contemporary political and social world was presented by the dramatist with such vividness that the hearer could forget his critical exhaustion and abandon himself to similar emotions, as, in patriotic or warlike moments, before the tribune of parliament, or at the condemnation of crime and vice:—an estrangement of the true aims of art which could not but lead directly now and then to a cult of tendency. But here there took place what has always taken place in the case of factitious arts, an extraordinary rapid depravation of these tendencies, so that for instance the tendency to employ the theatre as a means for the moral education of the people, which in Schiller's time was taken seriously, is already reckoned among the incredible antiquities of a surmounted culture. While the critic got the upper hand in the theatre and concert-hall, the journalist in the school, and the press in society, art degenerated into a topic of conversation of the most trivial kind, and æsthetic criticism was used as the cement of a vain, distracted, selfish and moreover piteously unoriginal sociality, the significance of which is suggested by the Schopenhauerian parable of the porcupines, so that there has never been so much gossip about art and so little esteem for it. But is it still possible to have intercourse with a man capable of conversing on Beethoven or Shakespeare? Let each answer this question according to his sentiments: he will at any rate show by his answer his conception of "culture," provided he tries at least to answer the question, and has not already grown mute with astonishment.

On the other hand, many a one more nobly and delicately endowed by nature, though he may have gradually become a critical barbarian in the manner described, could tell of the unexpected as well as totally unintelligible effect which a successful performance of *Lohengrin,* for example, exerted on him: except that perhaps every warning and interpreting hand was lacking to guide him; so that the incomprehensibly heterogeneous and altogether incomparable sensation which then affected him also remained isolated and became extinct, like a mysterious star after a brief brilliancy. He then divined what the æsthetic hearer is.

23.

He who wishes to test himself rigorously as to how he is related to the true æsthetic hearer, or whether he belongs rather to the community of the Socrato-critical man, has only to enquire sincerely concerning the sentiment with which he accepts the *wonder* represented on the stage: whether he feels his historical sense, which insists on strict psychological causality, insulted by it, whether with benevolent concession he as it were admits the wonder as a phenomenon intelligible to childhood, but relinquished by him, or whether he experiences anything else thereby. For he will thus be enabled to determine how far he is on the whole capable of understanding *myth,* that is to say, the concentrated picture of the world, which, as abbreviature of phenomena, cannot dispense with wonder. It is probable, however, that nearly every one, upon close examination, feels so disintegrated by the critico-historical spirit of our culture, that he can only perhaps make the former existence of myth credible to himself by learned means through intermediary abstractions. Without myth, however, every culture loses its healthy, creative natural power: it is only a horizon encompassed with myths which rounds off to unity a social movement. It is only by myth that all the powers of the imagination and of the Apollonian dream are freed from their random rovings. The mythical figures have to be the invisibly omnipresent genii, under the care of which the young soul grows to maturity, by the signs of which the man gives a meaning to his life and struggles: and the state itself knows no more powerful unwritten law than the mythical foundation which vouches for its connection with religion and its growth from mythical ideas.

Let us now place alongside thereof the abstract man proceeding independently of myth, the abstract education, the abstract usage, the abstract right, the abstract state: let us picture to ourselves the lawless roving of the artistic imagination, not bridled by any native myth: let us imagine a culture which has no fixed and sacred primitive seat, but is doomed to exhaust all its possibilities, and has to nourish itself wretchedly from the other cultures—

such is the Present, as the result of Socratism, which is bent on the destruction of myth. And now the myth-less man remains eternally hungering among all the bygones, and digs and grubs for roots, though he have to dig for them even among the remotest antiquities. The stupendous historical exigency of the unsatisfied modern culture, the gathering around one of countless other cultures, the consuming desire for knowledge—what does all this point to, if not to the loss of myth, the loss of the mythical home, the mythical source? Let us ask ourselves whether the feverish and so uncanny stirring of this culture is aught but the eager seizing and snatching at food of the hungerer—and who would care to contribute anything more to a culture which cannot be appeased by all it devours, and in contact with which the most vigorous and wholesome nourishment is wont to change into "history and criticism"?

We should also have to regard our German character with despair and sorrow, if it had already become inextricably entangled in, or even identical with this culture, in a similar manner as we can observe it to our horror to be the case in civilised France; and that which for a long time was the great advantage of France and the cause of her vast preponderance, to wit, this very identity of people and culture, might compel us at the sight thereof to congratulate ourselves that this culture of ours, which is so questionable, has hitherto had nothing in common with the noble kernel of the character of our people. All our hopes, on the contrary, stretch out longingly towards the perception that beneath this restlessly palpitating civilised life and educational convulsion there is concealed a glorious, intrinsically healthy, primeval power, which, to be sure, stirs vigorously only at intervals in stupendous moments, and then dreams on again in view of a future awakening. It is from this abyss that the German Reformation came forth: in the choral-hymn of which the future melody of German music first resounded. So deep, courageous, and soul-breathing, so exuberantly good and tender did this chorale of Luther sound,—as the first Dionysian-luring call which breaks forth from dense thickets at the approach of spring. To it responded with emulative echo the solemnly wanton procession of Dionysian revellers, to whom we are indebted for German music—and to whom we shall be indebted for *the re-birth of German myth.*

I know that I must now lead the sympathising and attentive friend to an elevated position of lonesome contemplation, where he will have but few companions, and I call out encouragingly to him that we must hold fast to our shining guides, the Greeks. For the rectification of our æsthetic knowledge we previously borrowed from them the two divine figures, each of which sways a separate realm of art, and concerning whose mutual contact and exaltation we have acquired a notion through Greek tragedy. Through a remarkable disruption of both these primitive artistic impulses, the ruin of Greek tragedy seemed to be necessarily brought about: with which process a degeneration and a transmutation of the Greek national character was strictly in keeping, summoning us to earnest reflection as to how closely and necessarily art and the people, myth and custom, tragedy and the state, have coalesced in their bases. The ruin of tragedy was at the same time the ruin of myth. Until then the Greeks had been involuntarily compelled immediately to associate all experiences with their myths, indeed they had to comprehend them only through this association: whereby even the most immediate present necessarily appeared to them *sub specie æterni* and in a certain sense as timeless. Into this current of the timeless, however, the state as well as art plunged in order to find repose from the burden and eagerness of the moment. And a people—for the rest, also a man—is worth just as much only as its ability to impress on its experiences the seal of eternity: for it is thus, as it were, desecularised, and reveals its unconscious inner conviction of the relativity of time and of the true, that is, the metaphysical significance of life. The contrary happens when a people begins to comprehend itself historically and to demolish the mythical bulwarks around it: with which there is usually connected a marked secularisation, a breach with the unconscious metaphysics of its earlier existence, in all ethical consequences. Greek art and especially Greek tragedy delayed above all the annihilation of myth: it was necessary to annihilate these also to be able to live detached from the native soil, unbridled in the wilderness of thought, custom, and action. Even in such circumstances this metaphysical impulse still endeavours to create for itself a form of apotheosis (weakened, no doubt) in the Socratism of science urging to life: but on its lower stage this same impulse led only to a feverish search, which gradually merged into a pandemonium of myths and superstitions accumulated from all quarters: in the midst of which, nevertheless, the Hellene sat with a yearning heart till he contrived, as Græculus, to mask his fever with Greek cheerfulness and Greek levity, or to narcotise himself completely with some gloomy Oriental superstition.

We have approached this condition in the most striking manner since the reawakening of the Alexandro—Roman antiquity in the fifteenth century, after a long, not easily describable, interlude. On the heights there is the same exuberant love of knowledge, the same insatiate happiness of the discoverer, the same stupendous secularisation, and, together with these, a homeless roving about, an eager intrusion at foreign tables, a frivolous deification of the present or a dull senseless estrangement, all *sub speci sæculi,* of the present time: which same symptoms lead one to infer the same defect at the heart of this culture, the annihilation of myth. It seems hardly possible to transplant a foreign myth with permanent success, without dreadfully injuring the tree through this transplantation: which is perhaps occasionally strong enough and sound enough to eliminate the foreign element after a terrible struggle; but must ordinarily consume itself in a languishing and stunted condition or in sickly luxuriance. Our opinion of the pure and vigorous kernel of the German being is such that we venture to expect of it, and only of it, this elimination of forcibly ingrafted foreign elements, and we deem it possible that the German spirit will reflect anew on itself. Perhaps many a one will be of opinion that this spirit must begin its struggle with the elimination of the Romanic element: for which it might recognise an external preparation and encouragement in the victorious bravery and bloody glory of the late war, but must seek the inner constraint in the emulative zeal to be for ever worthy of the sublime protagonists on this path, of Luther as well as our great artists and poets. But let him never think he can fight such battles without his household gods, without his mythical home, without a "restoration" of all German things I And if the German should look timidly around for a guide to lead him back to his long-lost home, the ways and paths of which he knows no longer—let him but listen to the delightfully luring call of the Dionysian bird, which hovers above him, and would fain point out to him the way thither.

24.

Among the peculiar artistic effects of musical tragedy we had to emphasise an Apollonian *illusion,* through which we are to be saved from immediate oneness with the Dionysian music, while our musical excitement is able to discharge itself on an Apollonian domain and in an interposed visible middle world. It thereby seemed to us that precisely through this discharge the middle world of theatrical procedure, the drama generally, became visible and intelligible from within in a degree unattainable in the other forms of Apollonian art: so that here, where this art was as it were winged and borne aloft by the spirit of music, we had to recognise the highest exaltation of its powers, and consequently in the fraternal union of Apollo and Dionysus the climax of the Apollonian as well as of the Dionysian artistic aims.

Of course, the Apollonian light-picture did not, precisely with this inner illumination through music, attain the peculiar effect of the weaker grades of Apollonian art. What the epos and the animated stone can do—constrain the contemplating eye to calm delight in the world of the *individuatio*—could not be realised here, notwithstanding the greater animation and distinctness. We contemplated the drama and penetrated with piercing glance into its inner agitated world of motives—and yet it seemed as if only a symbolic picture passed before us, the profoundest significance of which we almost believed we had divined, and which we desired to put aside like a curtain in order to behold the original behind it. The greatest distinctness of the picture did not suffice us: for it seemed to reveal as well as veil something; and while it seemed, with its symbolic revelation, to invite the rending of the veil for the disclosure of the mysterious background, this illumined all-conspicuousness itself enthralled the eye and prevented it from penetrating more deeply.

He who has not experienced this,—to have to view, and at the same time to have a longing beyond the viewing,—will hardly be able to conceive how clearly and definitely these two processes coexist in the contemplation of tragic myth and are felt to be conjoined; while the truly æsthetic spectators will confirm my assertion that among the peculiar effects of tragedy this conjunction is the most noteworthy. Now let this phenomenon of the æsthetic spectator be transferred to an analogous process in the tragic artist, and the genesis of *tragic myth* will have been understood. It shares with the Apollonian sphere of art the full delight in appearance and contemplation, and at the same time it denies this delight and finds a still higher satisfaction in the annihilation of the visible world of appearance. The substance of tragic myth is first of all an epic event involving the glorification of the fighting hero: but whence originates the essentially enigmatical trait, that the suffering in the fate of the hero, the most painful victories, the most agonising contrasts of motives, in short, the exemplification of the wisdom of Silenus, or, æsthetically expressed, the Ugly and Discordant, is always represented anew in such countless forms with such predilection, and precisely in the most youthful and exuberant age of a people, unless there is really a higher delight experienced in all this?

For the fact that things actually take such a tragic course would least of all explain the origin of a form of art; provided that art is not merely an imitation of the reality of nature, but in truth a metaphysical supplement to the reality of nature, placed alongside thereof for its conquest. Tragic myth, in so far as it really belongs to art, also fully participates in this transfiguring metaphysical purpose of art in general: What does it transfigure, however, when it presents the phenomenal world in the guise of the suffering hero? Least of all the "reality" of this phenomenal world, for it says to us: "Look at this! Look carefully! It is your life! It is the hour-hand of your clock of existence!"

And myth has displayed this life, in order thereby to transfigure it to us? If not, how shall we account for the æsthetic pleasure with which we make even these representations pass before us? I am inquiring concerning the æsthetic pleasure, and am well aware that many of these representations may moreover occasionally create even a moral delectation, say under the form of pity or of a moral triumph. But he who would derive the effect of the tragic exclusively from these moral sources, as was usually the case far too long in æsthetics, let him not think that he has done anything for Art thereby; for Art must above all insist on purity in her domain. For the explanation of tragic myth the very first requirement is that the pleasure which characterises it must be sought in the purely æsthetic sphere, without encroaching on the domain of pity, fear, or the morally-sublime. How can the ugly and the discordant, the substance of tragic myth, excite an æsthetic pleasure?

Here it is necessary to raise ourselves with a daring bound into a metaphysics of Art. I repeat, therefore, my former proposition, that it is only as an æsthetic phenomenon that existence and the world, appear justified: and in this sense it is precisely the function of tragic myth to convince us that even the Ugly and Discordant is an artistic game which the will, in the eternal fulness of its joy, plays with itself. But this not easily comprehensible proto-phenomenon of Dionysian Art becomes, in a direct way, singularly intelligible, and is immediately apprehended in the wonderful significance of *musical dissonance:* just as in general it is music alone, placed in contrast to the world, which can give us an idea as to what is meant by the justification of the world as an æsthetic phenomenon. The joy that the tragic myth excites has the same origin as the joyful sensation of dissonance in music. The Dionysian, with its primitive joy experienced in pain itself, is the common source of music and tragic myth.

Is it not possible that by calling to our aid the musical relation of dissonance, the difficult problem of tragic effect may have meanwhile been materially facilitated? For we now understand what it means to wish to view tragedy and at the same time to have a longing beyond the viewing: a frame of mind, which, as regards the artistically employed dissonance, we should simply have to characterise by saying that we desire to hear and at the same time have a longing beyond the hearing. That striving for the infinite, the pinion-flapping of longing, accompanying the highest delight in the clearly-perceived reality, remind one that in both states we have to recognise a Dionysian phenomenon, which again and again reveals to us anew the playful up-building and demolishing of the world of individuals as the efflux of a primitive delight, in like manner as when Heraclitus the Obscure compares the world-building power to a playing child which places stones here and there and builds sandhills only to overthrow them again.

Hence, in order to form a true estimate of the Dionysian capacity of a people, it would seem that we must think not only of their music, but just as much of their tragic myth, the second witness of this capacity. Considering this most intimate relationship between music and myth, we may now in like manner suppose that a degeneration and depravation of the one involves a deterioration of the other: if it be true at all that the weakening of the myth is generally expressive of a debilitation of the Dionysian capacity. Concerning both, however, a glance at the development of the German genius should not leave us in any doubt; in the opera just as in the abstract character of our myth-less existence, in an art sunk to pastime just as in a life guided by concepts, the inartistic as well as life-consuming nature of Socratic optimism had revealed itself to us. Yet there have been indications to console us that nevertheless in some inaccessible abyss the German spirit still rests and dreams, undestroyed, in glorious health, profundity, and Dionysian strength, like a knight sunk in slumber: from which abyss the Dionysian song rises to us to let us know that this German knight even still dreams his primitive Dionysian myth in blissfully earnest visions. Let no one believe that the German spirit has for ever lost its mythical home when it still understands so obviously the voices of the birds which tell of that home. Some day it will find itself awake in all the morning freshness of a deep sleep: then it will slay the dragons, destroy the malignant dwarfs, and waken Brünnhilde—and Wotan's spear itself will be unable to obstruct its course!

My friends, ye who believe in Dionysian music, ye know also what tragedy means to us. There we have tragic myth, born anew from music,—and in this latest birth ye can hope for everything and forget what is most afflicting. What is most afflicting to all of us, however, is—the prolonged degradation in which the German genius has lived estranged from house and home in the service of malignant dwarfs. Ye understand my allusion—as ye will also, in conclusion, understand my hopes.

25.

Music and tragic myth are equally the expression of the Dionysian capacity of a people, and are inseparable from each other. Both originate in an ultra Apollonian sphere of art; both transfigure a region in the delightful accords of which all dissonance, just like the terrible picture of the world, dies charmingly away; both play with the sting of displeasure, trusting to their most potent magic; both justify thereby the existence even of the "worst world." Here the Dionysian, as compared with the Apollonian, exhibits itself as the eternal and original artistic force, which in general calls into existence the entire world of phenomena: in the midst of which a new transfiguring appearance becomes necessary, in order to keep alive the animated world of individuation. If we could conceive an incarnation of dissonance—and what is man but that?—then, to be able to live this dissonance would require a glorious illusion which would spread a veil of beauty over its peculiar nature. This is the true function of Apollo as deity of art: in whose name we comprise all the countless manifestations of the fair realm of illusion, which each moment render life in general worth living and make one impatient for the experience of the next moment.

At the same time, just as much of this basis of all existence—the Dionysian substratum of the world—is allowed to enter into the consciousness of human beings, as can be surmounted again by the Apollonian transfiguring power, so that these two art-impulses are constrained to develop their powers in strictly mutual proportion, according to the law of eternal justice. When the Dionysian powers rise with such vehemence as we experience at present, there can be no doubt that, veiled in a cloud, Apollo has already descended to us; whose grandest beautifying influences a coming generation will perhaps behold.

That this effect is necessary, however, each one would most surely perceive by intuition, if once he found himself carried back—even in a dream—into an Old-Hellenic existence. In walking under high Ionic colonnades, looking upwards to a horizon defined by clear and noble lines, with reflections of his transfigured form by his side in shining marble, and around him solemnly marching or quietly moving men, with harmoniously sounding voices and rhythmical pantomime, would he not in the presence of this perpetual influx of beauty have to raise his hand to Apollo and exclaim: "Blessed race of Hellenes! How great Dionysus must be among you, when the Delian god deems such charms necessary to cure you of your dithyrambic madness!"—To one in this frame of mind, however, an aged Athenian, looking up to him with the sublime eye of Æschylus, might answer: "Say also this, thou curious stranger: what sufferings this people must have undergone, in order to be able to become thus beautiful! But now follow me to a tragic play, and sacrifice with me in the temple of both the deities!"

APPENDIX

[Late in the year 1888, not long before he was overcome by his sudden attack of insanity, Nietzsche wrote down a few notes concerning his early work, the *Birth of Tragedy.* These were printed in his sister's biography (*Das Leben Friedrich Nietzsches,* vol. ii. pt. i. pp. 102 ff.), and are here translated as likely to be of interest to readers of this remarkable work. They also appear in the *Ecce Homo.*—TRANSLATOR'S NOTE.]

"To be just to the *Birth of Tragedy*(1872), one will have to forget some few things. It has *wrought effects,* it even fascinated through that wherein it was amiss—through its application to *Wagnerism,* just as if this Wagnerism were symptomatic of *a rise and going up*. And just on that account was the book an event in Wagner's life: from thence and only from thence were great hopes linked to the name of Wagner. Even to-day people remind me, sometimes right in the midst of a talk on *Parsifal,* that *I*and none other have it on my conscience that such a high opinion of the *cultural value* of this movement came to the top. More than once have I found the book referred to as 'the *Re*-birth of Tragedy out of the Spirit of Music': one only had an ear for a new formula of *Wagner's* art, aim, task,—and failed to hear withal what was at bottom valuable therein. 'Hellenism and Pessimism' had been a more unequivocal title: namely, as a first lesson on the way in which the Greeks got the better of pessimism,—on the means whereby they *overcame* it. Tragedy simply proves that the Greeks were *no* pessimists: Schopenhauer was mistaken here as he was mistaken in all other things. Considered with some neutrality, the *Birth of Tragedy* appears very unseasonable: one would not even dream that it was *begun* amid the thunders of the battle of Wörth. I thought these problems through and through before the walls of Metz in cold September nights, in the midst of the work of nursing the sick; one might even believe the book to be fifty years older. It is politically indifferent—un-German one will say to-day,—it smells shockingly Hegelian, in but a few formulæ does it scent of Schopenhauer's funereal perfume. An 'idea'—the antithesis of 'Dionysian *versus* Apollonian'—translated into metaphysics; history itself as the evolution of this 'idea'; the antithesis dissolved into oneness in Tragedy; through this optics things that had never yet looked into one another's face, confronted of a sudden, and illumined and *comprehended* through one another: for instance, Opera and Revolution. The two decisive *innovations* of the book are, on the one hand, the comprehension of the *Dionysian* phenomenon among the Greeks (it gives the first psychology thereof, it sees therein the One root of all Grecian art); on the other, the comprehension of Socratism: Socrates diagnosed for the first time as the tool of Grecian dissolution, as a typical decadent. 'Rationality' *against* instinct! 'Rationality' at any price as a dangerous, as a life-undermining force! Throughout the whole book a deep hostile silence on Christianity: it is neither Apollonian nor Dionysian; it *negatives* all *æsthetic* values (the only values recognised by the *Birth of Tragedy),* it is in the widest sense nihilistic, whereas in the Dionysian symbol the utmost limit of *affirmation* is reached. Once or twice the Christian priests are alluded to as a 'malignant kind of dwarfs,' as 'subterraneans.'"

2.

"This beginning is singular beyond measure. I had for my own inmost experience *discovered* the only symbol and counterpart of history,—I had just thereby been the first to grasp the wonderful phenomenon of the Dionysian. And again, through my diagnosing Socrates as a decadent, I had given a wholly unequivocal proof of how little risk the trustworthiness of my psychological grasp would run of being weakened by some moralistic idiosyncrasy—to view morality itself as a symptom of decadence is an innovation, a novelty of the first rank in the history of knowledge. How far I had leaped in either case beyond the smug shallow-pate-gossip of optimism *contra* pessimism! I was the first to see the intrinsic antithesis: here, the *degenerating* instinct which, with subterranean vindictiveness, turns against life (Christianity, the philosophy of Schopenhauer, in a certain sense already the philosophy of Plato, all idealistic systems as typical forms), and there, a formula of *highest affirmation,* born of fullness and overfullness, a yea-saying without reserve to suffering's self, to guilt's self, to all that is questionable and strange in existence itself. This final, cheerfullest, exuberantly mad-and-merriest Yea to life is not only the highest insight, it is also the *deepest,* it is that which is most rigorously confirmed and upheld by truth and science. Naught that is, is to be deducted, naught is dispensable; the phases of existence rejected by the Christians and other nihilists are even of an infinitely higher order in the hierarchy of values than that which the instinct of decadence sanctions, yea durst *sanction.* To comprehend this *courage* is needed, and, as a condition thereof, a surplus of *strength*: for precisely in degree as courage *dares* to thrust forward, precisely according to the measure of strength, does one approach truth. Perception, the yea-saying to reality, is as much a necessity to the strong as to the weak, under the inspiration of weakness, cowardly shrinking, and *flight* from reality—the 'ideal.' ... They are not free to perceive: the decadents have *need* of the lie,—it is one of their conditions of self-preservation. Whoso not only comprehends the word Dionysian, but also grasps his *self* in this word, requires no refutation of Plato or of Christianity or of Schopenhauer—*he smells the putrefaction.*"

3.

"To what extent I had just thereby found the concept 'tragic,' the definitive perception of the psychology of tragedy, I have but lately stated in the *Twilight of the Idols,* page 139 (1st edit.): 'The affirmation of life, even in its most unfamiliar and severe problems, the will to life, enjoying its own inexhaustibility in the sacrifice of its highest types,—*that* is what I called

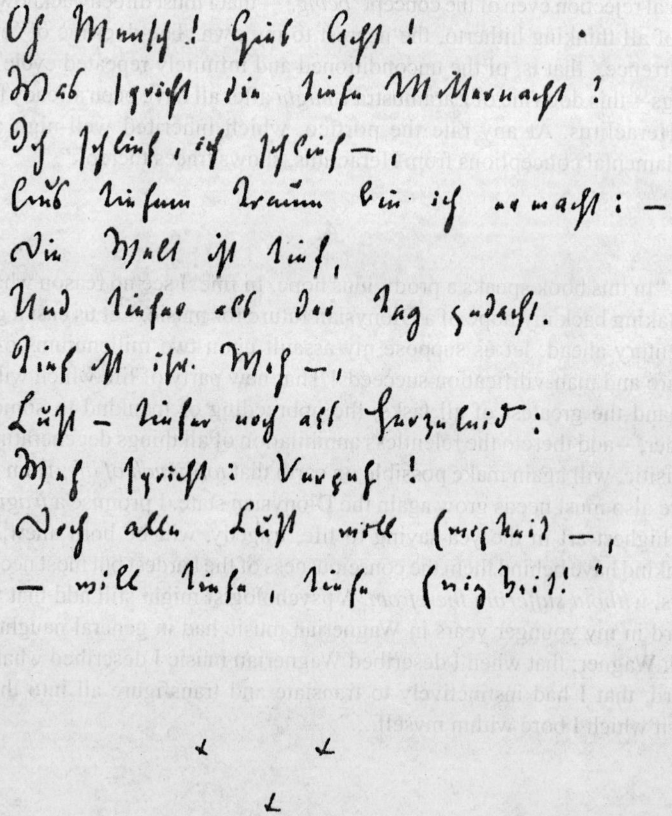
Oh Mensch! Gib Acht!
Was spricht die tiefe Mitternacht?
„Ich schlief, ich schlief —,
„Aus tiefem Traum bin ich erwacht: —
„Die Welt ist tief,
„Und tiefer als der Tag gedacht.
„Tief ist ihr Weh —,
„Lust — tiefer noch als Herzeleid:
„Weh spricht: Vergeh!
„Doch alle Lust will Ewigkeit —,
„— will tiefe, tiefe Ewigkeit!"

Dionysian, that is what I divined as the bridge to a psychology of the *tragic* poet. Not in order to get rid of terror and pity, not to purify from a dangerous passion by its vehement discharge (it was thus that Aristotle misunderstood it); but, beyond terror and pity, *to realise in fact* the eternal delight of becoming, that delight which even involves in itself the *joy of annihilating!** In this sense I have the right to understand myself to be the first *tragic philosopher*—that

* Mr. Common's translation, pp. 227-28.

is, the utmost antithesis and antipode to a pessimistic philosopher. Prior to myself there is no such translation of the Dionysian into the philosophic pathos: there lacks the *tragic wisdom,*—I have sought in vain for an indication thereof even among the *great* Greeks of philosophy, the thinkers of the two centuries *before* Socrates. A doubt still possessed me as touching *Heraclitus,* in whose proximity I in general begin to feel warmer and better than anywhere else. The affirmation of transiency *and annihilation,* to wit the decisive factor in a Dionysian *philosophy,* the yea-saying to antithesis and war, to *becoming,* with radical rejection even of the concept '*being,*'—that I must directly acknowledge as, of all thinking hitherto, the nearest to my own. The doctrine of 'eternal recurrence,' that is, of the unconditioned and infinitely repeated cycle of all things—this doctrine of Zarathustra's *might* after all have been already taught by Heraclitus. At any rate the portico, which inherited well-nigh all its fundamental conceptions from Heraclitus, shows traces thereof."

4.

"In this book speaks a prodigious hope. In fine, I see no reason whatever for taking back my hope of a Dionysian future for music. Let us cast a glance a century ahead, let us suppose my assault upon two millenniums of anti-nature and man-vilification succeeds! That new party of life which will take in hand the greatest of all tasks, the upbreeding of mankind to something higher,—add thereto the relentless annihilation of all things degenerating and parasitic, will again make possible on earth that *too-much of life,* from which there also must needs grow again the Dionysian state. I promise a *tragic* age: the highest art in the yea-saying to life, tragedy, will be born anew, when mankind have behind them the consciousness of the hardest but most necessary wars, *without suffering therefrom.* A psychologist might still add that what I heard in my younger years in Wagnerian music had in general naught to do with Wagner; that when I described Wagnerian music I described what *I* had heard, that I had instinctively to translate and transfigure all into the new spirit which I bore within myself...."

TRANSLATOR'S NOTE

While the translator flatters himself that this version of Nietzsche's early work—having been submitted to unsparingly scrutinising eyes—is not altogether unworthy of the original, he begs to state that he holds twentieth-century English to be a rather unsatisfactory vehicle for philosophical thought. Accordingly, in conjunction with his friend Dr. Ernest Lacy, he has prepared a second, more unconventional translation,—in brief, a translation which will enable one whose knowledge of English extends to, say, the period of Elizabeth, to appreciate Nietzsche in more forcible language, because the language of a stronger age. It is proposed to provide this second translation with an appendix, containing many references to the translated writings of Wagner and Schopenhauer; to the works of Pater, Browning, Burckhardt, Rohde, and others, and a summmary and index.

For help in preparing the present translation, the translator wishes to express his thanks to his friends Dr. Ernest Lacy, Litt.D.; Dr. James Waddell Tupper, Ph.D.; Prof. Harry Max Ferren; Mr. James M'Kirdy, Pittsburg; and Mr. Thomas Common, Edinburgh.

WILLIAM AUGUST HAUSSMANN, A.B., Ph.D.